# FORTRAN IV
## *A Modern Approach*

# FORTRAN IV
# *A Modern Approach*

## Frank D. Vickers
University of Florida

**HOLT, RINEHART AND WINSTON, INC.**
*New York   Chicago   San Francisco   Atlanta*
*Dallas   Montreal   Toronto   London   Sydney*

ISBN: 0-03-083060-5

Printed in the United States of America

12345  005  98765432

# Preface

A great many books have been written on computers, computer programming, and computer programming languages, particularly Fortran. To produce another book on Fortran, even the newest Fortran IV, probably seems unreasonable to most, and it is with mild trepidation that the author embarks on this project. However, several good reasons can be stated for doing just that. Most computer professionals will agree that the field of computer and information science has quickly become a valid discipline for academia, and that rapid changes are occurring in computer programming languages. Both of these facts demand that a new direction be taken in presenting the subject.

This text is designed to meet these demands by using new techniques in a context different from previous manuals on programming. There is a great deal more to the appreciation of computing systems than merely knowing a programming language. The approach here is to serve the needs of new students in the computer sciences, whether in college, junior college, technical institute, or high school.

To avoid limiting the subject matter or the student's understanding of it, it is recommended that this book be used in a course at least four quarter hours or three semester hours in length. The major misunderstanding of most teachers and students of programming is that they think programming is simple and can be learned quickly. This is untrue. The primary ingredient of good programming is experience, and experience requires individual effort over an extended period of time. Furthermore, this course should be followed by a course concerning assembly languages in order to bring home the real meaning and power of higher-level languages.

To meet these requirements the following ideas, some innovative, are incorporated into the book:

1. An introductory chapter concerning modern concepts in computer operation is included to orient the student to the broad range of computer environments.
2. Emphasis is placed on fundamentals throughout the book, but particularly in the first few chapters. A firm foundation is established, so that the student can grow in knowledge and learn to adapt to a rapidly changing field.
3. Subject matter is presented in an order based on experience gained in over ten years of teaching the material. This sequence seems to be nearly optimal, producing maximum appreciation of the subject.
4. The analysis of algorithms is presented through simplified discussions of certain programs placed at appropriate points throughout the text.
5. The introduction to syntactic and semantic description of computer languages provides the student with some background for future courses involving mechanical linguistics.
6. The examples chosen for illustration are not slanted toward any one discipline. Anyone should be able to understand every example used.
7. The book also uses some special editorial techniques to

maximize the learning experience. These include boxing all pertinent definitions for emphasis, easy reference, and easy review. The same examples are used in several chapters to provide continuity and to show how a concept can be expanded as understanding of the subject grows. Also, the correspondence between program segments and pictorial flow charts is shown by parallel presentation. A limited number of comprehensive examples is used to reduce impedimenta. Most illustrations are given by short program segments. Complete programs are shown only where they serve a major purpose.

8. Finally, the major goal is to teach the concepts and mental thought patterns which are needed for proper understanding of computing and for the process of creating computing procedures.

The author wishes to acknowledge the contributions made by the many students he has taught. It must also be recognized that the University of Florida and some of its faculty members provided a unique laboratory for the development of the concepts used within this text. Appreciation must be expressed to R. H. Wessels for his help in bringing the ideas into reality. Special thanks is given to the author's wife, who aided in the preparation of the manuscript, and who pointed out that English also has a syntax.

*June, 1970*                                                       F. D. Vickers
*Gainesville, Florida*

# Contents

# Definitions

**Definitions** *(cont'd)*

**Definitions** *(cont'd)*

**Definitions** *(cont'd)*

**Definitions** *(cont'd)*

CHAPTER **1**

# Generalized Concepts in Modern Computing Systems

## 1.1 INTRODUCTION

The science of computers and the technology of their use are broad, complex subjects made even more so by a very rapid rate of change. Like other similar fields, computer science is replete with its own terminology and jargon. Here, in this chapter, an attempt will be made to cast some light on a few of the very basic terms and concepts that should be of interest to the prospective computer user.

| 1.1 Computer |
| --- |
| A computer is a device which, when properly instructed by way of a program, will perform useful computations automatically at high speed. |

There are several types of computers. Within each type there are many machines of different size and speed. The concern here will be with the digital type of computer: more specifically, a digital computer of general purpose and, primarily, one with speed of computation measured in microseconds.

Digital computers are of a general class of machine that can perform computations and manipulations involving digits, much as you might with pencil and paper, but with much higher speed and reliability. In more simple terms they add, subtract, multiply, and divide numbers. In addition, they provide for making comparisons and logical decisions, provisions which are prerequisite for automatic operation.

Definition 1.1 should be discussed further, particularly with reference to the computer performing useful computation. This obviously is highly desirable, but it depends inexorably upon the computer being properly instructed. The computer user, herein referred to as a programmer, must be constantly prepared to face the fact that what goes into a computer comes out, and that includes garbage. In other words, the computer does only what it is told to do, no more and no less. If the machine is instructed to make an erroneous computation, it does so without a second thought. A very good description of a computer is, "It is a fantastically fast moron."

---

### 1.2 Program

A program is a set of detailed, specific, and precise instructions written in a specified form and language by the programmer for use by a computer to solve a given problem.

---

The first major hurdle standing before the prospective computer programmer is best described as a language barrier. The various languages the computer understands are more or less strange to people. However, these languages are much more precise in structure and less complicated in scope than natural languages, such as English or German. Thus the student should find it much easier to learn a computer language than to learn to speak, read, and write in a language other than his native tongue.

The second major hurdle the new programmer must face can be likened to that faced by a poet or novelist. Knowing a language does not mean that one can write good poetry or a good novel. It does take experience and some undetermined amount and quality of talent. The same appears to be true of programming, for one does not write good programs just by knowing a computer language.

The programmer must be good at performing four basic steps:

1.  The formulation and understanding of the problem to be solved;
2.  The appreciation of how the problem should be solved in terms of the capabilities and limitations of the computer;
3.  The translation and implementation of the solution procedure into a program written in a particular computer language;
4.  The verification of the solution.

Many times the programmer finds at Step 4 that he must recycle through one or more of the other steps before he can obtain acceptable answers.

It has not yet been proven, but the author suspects, that good programmers have certain personality traits which are unique and unfortunately appear to be somewhat rare in the general population.

In general these seem to be:

1.  A logical mind,
2.  A good short-term memory,
3.  A respect for details,
4.  A compulsive drive to perfection,
5.  A persistence in the face of failure.

Thus, learning to be a good computer programmer is a multifaceted task. To make this task as simple as possible and yet to make it rewarding, one particular computer language has been chosen to work with throughout this text. At present this language is very popular among computer users. Since it is the most prevalent language, it can be found in most computer installations.

Further discussion of Definition 1.2 may be helpful at this point. A program is a set of:

1. Detailed instructions in the sense that every movement that the computer is to make, during the process of solving a problem, must be spelled out completely.
2. Specific instructions that must be chosen from among a specified group of possible valid instructions.
3. Precise instructions in which every detail must be precisely correct in order to yield a valid solution.

---

1.3 Fortran IV

Fortran IV, acronym for formula translator, is a specific computer programming language known for the ease with which it can be learned and for its applicablity to scientific problems.

---

The source of the name Fortran is the key to its simplicity. Algebraic expressions and equations involved in the solution to a problem can be written into Fortran with only minor changes from the form with which most people are familiar. There are certain rules and limitations the programmer must abide by, but they are relatively easy to live with. The language only becomes complicated and more difficult to deal with when control, input and output, and decision-making features are added.

Detailed presentation of the Fortran language will begin in Chapter 2. However, as a brief introduction, a simple Fortran program is shown here for illustration. The program reads into the computer two values, A and B. The sum and the difference are computed, and the results, together with input data, are written as output. The program then repeats itself for as many sets of A and B as the programmer provides in the input data stream.

```
1    READ, A, B
     SUM = A + B
     DIF = A — B
     PRINT, A, B, SUM, DIF
     GO TO 1
     END
```

## 1.2 COMPUTER ORGANIZATION

To be able to discuss intelligently the operation of various computer systems in later sections, we present a brief discussion of the typical aspects of the physical organization of computer systems.

| 1.4 Hardware |
| --- |
| Hardware is the word that describes all of the various physical devices which make up a computer. |

| 1.5 Software |
| --- |
| Software describes the programs which are written by the manufacturer and/or local users to be executed by the hardware. |

There are many variations of the definitions given in 1.4 through 1.6, but the general ones presented here will suit our purpose. Definitions 1.7 through 1.10 describe in more detail the organization of the hardware shown in Figure 1.1. Section

1.3 will discuss in more detail the computing system as a whole and the software/hardware interdependence in general.

---

### 1.6 Computing System

In this text, a computing system will be considered the hardware supplied by the manufacturer together with the software written by the manufacturer and user to provide a composite operating system.

---

### 1.7 Central Processor

The central processor, or central processing unit (CPU), of the computer is the device which performs the program-indicated operations. These operations include add, subtract, multiply, divide, compare two numbers, and branch to location one. Also, this unit maintains control over all the other units in the system.

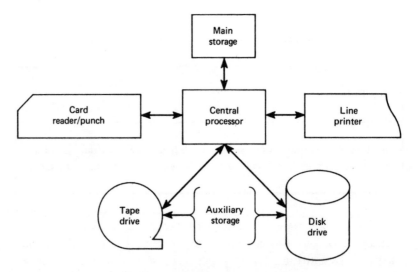

**Figure 1.1 Hardware organization.**

---

1.8 Main Storage

---

The main storage is that part of the computer where the program resides during its execution. In computer science terminology, this is referred to as the stored program principle. Data for the problem may also reside here.

---

1.9 Input/Output Devices

---

Input and output devices provide the communication link between the computer and the outside world. They include such devices as card readers and punches, line printers, typewriters, paper-tape readers and punches, and so on.

---

1.10 Auxiliary Storage

---

Auxiliary storage units are usually larger than the main storage unit but access to them is slower. Jobs waiting to be processed can be stored here. Auxiliary storage devices include magnetic tapes, disks, drums, and data cells.

Actually, computer hardware devices are much more diverse and complicated than these definitions might imply. A great deal is involved in the design and manufacture of computer equipment and involves a part of the total field of computer science; however, any further discussion at this point is beyond the scope of this book.

## 1.3 COMPUTER OPERATION

There are many different environments in which computers are operated. Generally speaking, they are referred to as being open or closed shop, batch-mode, multiprogramming, and time-sharing; these encompass remote job entry and conversational operation, as well as many others. In this section, some of these terms are defined and the pros and cons of each are discussed.

---

1.11 Open Shop

---

An open-shop computer environment is one in which any one user may gain direct "hands-on" access to *all* of the computer equipment at one time.

---

Open-shop computer operation (Figure 1.2) is gratifying for the individual programmer once he gains access, provided that time is not a factor and that only a reasonable number of people want access to the machine. From the viewpoint of

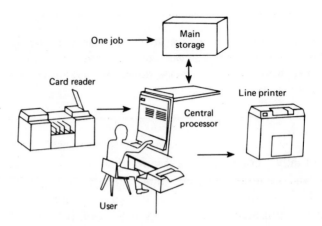

**Figure 1.2 Open shop computing system.**

computer operation, however, an open shop is very inefficient because inevitably a great deal of time is wasted, both during a programmer's sojourn on the machine and between visits by different people.

This type of operation is feasible only when the machine is small scale, is relatively inexpensive, and has relatively small user demand. Some people feel the inefficiency is not too high a price to pay for the "hands-on" experience, but this author feels that this attitude is unrealistic for the simple reason that the bulk of scientific computing is done in closed shop computing centers. It seems more reasonable to train programmers in the use of systems that they are more likely to encounter in their careers.

---

**1.12 Closed Shop**

A closed-shop computer environment is one in which actual computer operation is maintained by trained operators in order to increase efficiency.

---

In order to improve the efficiency of the computing system, we must enable it to accomplish more work in a given length of time. When control of the computer is limited to a group of trained computer operators, jobs can be collected from the users and run in succession with a minimim of confusion and delay between jobs. See Figure 1.3.

---

**1.13 Batch-Mode Shop**

The batch-mode form of computer operation is usually characterized by the placing of job queuing control under the computer itself through the use of a monitor system. This further improves efficiency.

---

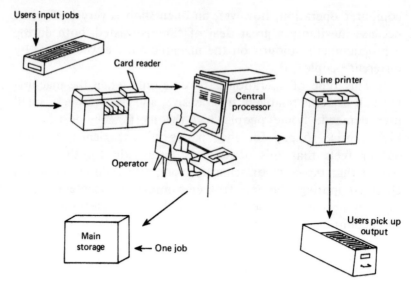

**Figure 1.3 Closed shop computing system.**

Batch-mode operation is an extension of the simple closed-shop concept discussed above. Here the control of transfer from one job to the next has, for the most part, been removed from the human operator's responsibility to improve efficiency even more. See Figure 1.4. The operator has the power to intervene in the process, but does so only under unusual conditions.

This type of operation is made possible by use of an auxiliary storage device, such as a tape or a disk memory unit, to maintain control over the user-input job queue and user-output queue within the machine itself. Thus the computer can control the transition from one job to the next without constant manual intervention.

---

1.14 Multiprogramming Shop

---

A multiprogramming computer environment provides the means to run several jobs concurrently; it improves efficiency by utilizing time which would be idle in a nonmultiprogramming system.

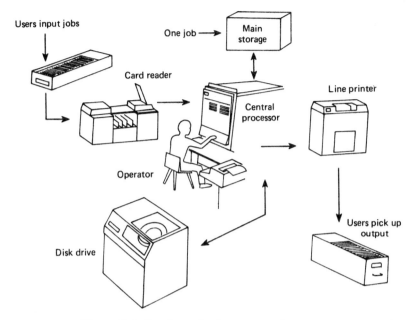

**Figure 1.4 Batch-mode shop computing system.**

Under normal circumstances, while a program is being executed, there are times when the central processor is forced to wait. For example, if data is requested by an executing program, time is required to obtain that data from either the auxiliary storage device or the card reader. During this time the central processor is idle. We improve efficiency by providing means to execute several jobs concurrently, thus using some of the idle time. This does not mean, however, that programs are executed simultaneously.

Another important point is that the operation of slow-speed card readers, punches, line printers, and so forth can be controlled as separate tasks without appreciable effect on the user job being executed. Thus higher efficiency is obtained. See Figure 1.5.

Physically adding a number of remote terminals, which consist of typewriter keyboards and/or card-reading equipment, to a computer system operating in a multiprogramming environment, enables us to devise new modes of computer operation. These time-sharing operations bring with them interesting advantages over more simple systems. See Figure 1.6.

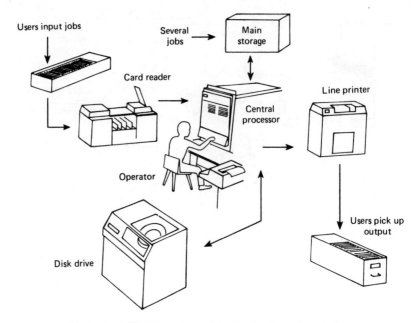

**Figure 1.5 Multiprogramming shop computing system.**

---

1.15 Time-Sharing Shop

---

A time-sharing operation is a relatively new type of environment characterized by several remote, user-oriented terminals appended to a multiprogramming system.

---

1.16 Foreground-Background Operation

---

The foreground-background operation is characteristic of a composite time-sharing and batch-mode system. Normally, the batch-mode operation is said to be operating in the background, while "conversations" between the computer and the remote terminal users are said to be operating in the foreground.

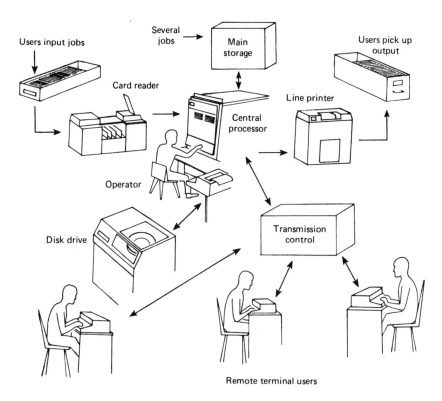

**Figure 1.6  Time-sharing shop computing system.**

Experience has shown that many jobs destined for computer solution do not require the special attention or services obtainable with remote terminals. Thus the procedures of batch-mode job submission should be retained regardless of how sophisticated a computing system may become. The use of multiprogramming enables service programs designed to support the remote terminals (and provide terminal users with specialized and generalized services) to operate during time when the central processor normally would be idle. More efficient use of the computing resources is thus obtained.

When the foreground users are given priority, conversations can be maintained between these remote users and the computing system; this allows implementation of many new and interesting features in the time-sharing system, some of which are listed here for illustration:

---

### 1.17 Conversational Operation

The conversational mode of operation is the almost natural communication that can be sustained, between a remote user and the computer, with no appreciable delay between user-input messages and computer-output responses.

---

1. Files of *programs* can be built up by the user, and cataloged, retrieved, listed, edited, or executed.
2. Files of *data* can be entered, manipulated, edited, or listed.
3. The computer can be used to teach through a stimulus-response technique called Computer Assisted Instruction.
4. Programs can be executed in the foreground in such a way that the user can observe and control their progress. This is especially useful in debugging and checking out a new program, or in guiding the computer in the solution of a problem that requires human interaction.
5. The computer remote terminal can be used as a desk calculator; this mode of operation provides the accessibility of a desk calculator linked to the power of a large computer.

---

### 1.18 Remote Job Entry

Remote job entry is simply the action of remotely entering the commands, program, and data that are necessary to submit a job into the background job stream.

Remote job entry is a compromise operation which combines the convenience of a remote terminal with the efficiency of the batch-mode computer operation. It lacks the advantage of conversational interaction with the program during its execution.

In a remote job entry environment, programs and data may be entered manually from the remote keyboard or locally through the batch-mode queue. In either event, the files of programs and/or data may be stored permanently on auxiliary storage devices for later retrieval and use. These files can then be retrieved, manipulated, modified or edited, listed, executed, and so on.

Computer operating efficiency is measured in several ways. Two common indices are called "throughput" and "turnaround time."

---

### 1.19 Throughput

Throughput is a measure of the amount of actual computation (that is, the number of jobs run) performed in a given length of time.

---

### 1.20 Turnaround Time

Turnaround time is that wall-clock time which elapses between initial submission of a computer job by the user and return of results to the user.

---

These two measures are viewed differently by the user and the computer manager. The goals of the two measures conflict. It may not be obvious at first, but an improvement in one measure will, in general, cause a degradation in the other. Closer examination clarifies this point.

From the computer manager's viewpoint, throughput should be increased to yield greater return on his investment. Progression from an open to a closed shop increases throughput, while, on the other hand, the turnaround time degrades.

From the user's viewpoint, turnaround should be decreased, to give him more work for his time. Progression from an open to a closed shop increases turnaround time, to the frustration of the user.

The same conflict exists with the more sophisticated batch-mode and multiprogrammed environments. Each of these refinements in system operation is designed to increase and improve throughput. This is necessary in a computing system which must grow to keep up with user demands. Implementing these refinements usually increases turnaround time, and thus degrades the user response. To counteract the degradation and improve turnaround, time-sharing with its conversational ability is being implemented in a great many large computing centers.

It should be obvious by now that computer utilization is complex; and trade-offs between throughput and turnaround must be made. Large computing center management and control has become a science unto itself.

Another, less obvious advantage of time-sharing with remote terminals, is the removal of a portion of the work load being placed on the card readers and line printers. In a non-time-sharing environment, the input/output equipment can become overloaded. This state is referred to as being input/output bound. On the other hand, with a large number of remote terminals in operation, the computer's central processor tends to become overloaded. This state is referred to as being compute bound. Thus, the total computing system must be designed, balanced, and tuned to meet all of these demands in an effective, yet efficient manner.

One final point should be made in connection with time-shared computing systems. Due to the high-speed capability of the large central processor relative to the slow speeds of typewriter keyboards and their human operators, the individual user of a good time-sharing system can assume the feeling that he is the sole user of the computer. While this is pleasant and conducive to work and accomplishment, it is, perhaps, wise to be aware that one is not working alone.

Time-sharing systems are very new and very complex; and they can sometimes be unreliable. The design, implementation, and checking out of such systems is extremely challenging and must also be done by human programmers.

## 1.4 FORTRAN OPERATION

In the context of Sections 1 through 3, we can now present two popular concepts of how a Fortran program can be processed. These two concepts are called compilation and interpretation. Before defining each of these, we need one more definition.

---

1.21 Machine Language

---

Machine language is a very peculiar, yet necessary, computer language which is basically the only language the computer understands.

---

It can be seen from Definition 1.21, that something must be done about Fortran, since it cannot be comprehended by the machine standing alone. Therefore, a problem of language translation exists. The problem is solved by introducing the concept of compilation.

---

1.22 Compilation

---

Compilation is a language translation operation to be performed by the computer itself.

---

1.23 Fortran Compiler

---

A Fortran compiler is a program existing in machine language that, while being executed by the computer, will cause a Fortran program to be translated into machine language.

---

---

1.24 Fortran Source Program

---

A Fortran source program is the initial program written by the user, and is input data to the compiler.

---

---

1.25 Object Program

---

The object program is the output from the Fortran compiler and is the machine language version or translation of the Fortran source program.

---

Thus, when a Fortran program is written and submitted to the computer by the user, the source program is first translated into an object program by the compiler. Then, if requested, it is executed to produce the results, provided that the original source program and data required are correct. These two operations are usually considered to be separable and are referred to as the compilation phase or source time, and the execution phase or object time. These two operations are shown in Figure 1.7.

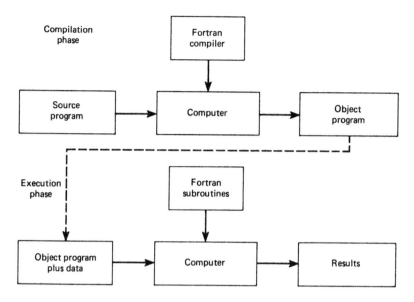

**Figure 1.7 Fortran IV compilation procedure.**

Most Fortran systems allow these two phases to be performed either together as one job or as separate jobs with any amount of time elapsing between. This allows programs to be compiled one day and executed another. Also, an object program can be executed many times on many days without being recompiled, thus saving machine time.

The Fortran compiler and its associated routines are available in either the batch-mode or the remote job entry types of computer operation. Normally, this type of system is not available as a conversational system and does not provide all the advantages of the interpretation concept discussed next.

---

1.26 Interpretation

Interpretation is an intermixing of translation and execution, usually to the point where the two are no longer distinguishable.

1.27 Fortran Interpreter

The Fortran interpreter is a program, existing in machine language, which, while being executed, will cause a Fortran program to be translated and executed to produce results without production of the intermediate object program.

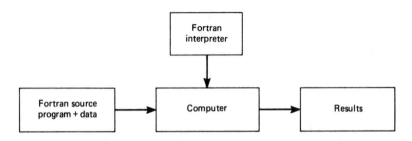

**Figure 1.8 Fortran IV interpretation procedure.**

The interpretation concept of Fortran operation (Figure 1.8) implemented within a conversational environment provides for new abilities which yield certain advantages over other systems. The major improvements are:

1. Conversational execution with user observation;
2. Retention of the source program which provides a direct link between error conditions and the source language most familiar to the user;
3. Diagnostic capability allowing error correction without recompilation;
4. Absence of need to have programs initially complete in every detail, as in a compilation run.

It seems that the interpreter has all the advantages, but not so. A program is executed much more slowly by an interpreter than the same program can be compiled and executed. Thus an interpreter is primarily a diagnostic tool. Production work should be accomplished with a compiler. One additional advantage of the interpreter is its educational value. It is felt that the student gains valuable experience in programming by observing programs in execution under an interpreter system.

## PRACTICE EXERCISES

1.1 A phrase often heard around computing centers and among computer programmers is, "garbage in—garbage out." What does this phrase mean?

1.2 Try writing a set of detailed instructions for doing a common daily task, such as getting up in the morning or another seemingly simple task.

1.3 List the four general divisions of computer hardware and discuss how they interact.

1.4 Given the following types of computer operation: open shop, closed shop, batch-mode, and multiprogramming shop.
   (a) Rank these operations for efficiency from the viewpoint of the computer user.
   (b) Do the same from the viewpoint of the computing center manager.

1.5 What is the major difference between Figures 1.4 and 1.5? How does this yield an improvement in machine operation efficiency?

1.6 Explain the effects on throughput and turnaround the following changes in an open shop would have: (a) the placing of computer control in the hands of trained operators, (b) the further addition of computerized job queuing, (c) the further utilization of idle CPU time, and (d) finally the addition of remote terminals.

1.7 Carl Moonlight is a computer operations manager for a large computing center. Jimmy Electron is a scientific programmer who makes frequent use of the same computing system. At exactly 5:01PM both are seen leaving the computing center, Carl looking very pleased with himself while Jimmy looks very grim. Assuming their moods are due to the behavior of the computer, explain in terms described in this chapter what this behavior must be.

1.8 The text has stated that throughput improves and turnaround degrades in going from an open shop to a batch-mode shop and also in going from a batch-mode to a multiprogramming shop. How can turnaround increase if jobs are being executed more quickly? *Hint:* Think in terms of job queue length and the total time spent by jobs residing within a system.

1.9 Describe two methods of processing Fortran jobs and explain the necessity of the translation involved.

1.10 How many languages can a computer understand without the benefit of any outside aid?

1.11 What is Fortran IV and what are some of its characteristics?

1.12 Define hardware and software as they are associated with computer operations.

1.13 One often hears of computers referred to as "electronic brains." What parts of a complex computer system might be considered the actual "brain"? What would be a better analogy?

1.14 Describe the interrelation of machine language, the Fortran compiler, and the Fortran source and object programs.

# CHAPTER 2

# Language
# Fundamentals and
# Arithmetic Operations

## 2.1 INTRODUCTION

Fortran IV is a language but unlike most natural languages it has a structure which is both simple and precise, with relatively few exceptions to rules of grammar. More specifically, Fortran IV is a computer programming language. Because of its simple and precise structure, and because of its ability to be translated, it is sometimes referred to as a mechanical or artificial language, as opposed to a natural language such as English. Nevertheless, the discussion of Fortran IV will develop much as a discussion of a natural language.

There are several approaches to the teaching of Fortran I V. It is felt the best approach is to construct a firm foundation of the principles and basic structure of the language. Upon this footing more meaningful discussions of the use of the language can then be based. Thus, this chapter will start at the bottom of the language structure and begin to ascend through the various levels of language complexity.

## 2.2 THE LANGUAGE ALPHABET

The characters (graphic marks or objects) used in the alphabet of Fortran IV are the same as those of English but have a somewhat different set of meanings assigned to them. The total character set is shown in Definition 2.1.

---

2.1 Basic Character Set of Fortran IV

---

ABCDEFGHIJKLMNOPQRSTUVWXYZ$0123456789+−*/=.(),'&
and the *blank.*
There is no other meaning, other than physical.

---

The *blank* is also considered a basic character. No special meanings are applied to these basic characters at this point, except that they represent forty-nine unique graphical objects.

It will become apparent throughout the development of Fortran IV, that each element of the language, other than those in Definition 2.1, will have a clear-cut logical as well as physical meaning. In the vernacular of the mechanical linguist, these two meanings are distinguished as follows. The physical or syntactic meaning of an element refers to its graphical characteristics, or simply how it looks. The logical or semantic meaning of an element refers to its actual meaning which, in terms of computer behavior, indicates the computation to be accomplished. A third meaning in linguistics, and of least importance to us here, is the pragmatics of the element, which has to do with when and where the final meaning is determined. In other words, a program might mean one thing one day and something else the next day. Obviously, this possibility is somewhat frightening. Fortunately, in the case of Fortran IV such ambiguities do not occur often. A more frequent result is that the same program means something different in one computing shop than it does in another.

It is suggested that a strong attempt be made to appreciate both of the denotations given in each of the following definitions. Each definition box is divided into three partitions: term being defined, physical meaning, and logical meaning.

---

**2.2 Alphabetic or Letter Characters**

---

**ABCDEFGHIJKLMNOPQRSTUVWXYZ$**

---

A subset of the basic character set.

---

**2.3 Numeric or Digit Characters**

---

**0123456789**

---

A subset of the basic character set, different from 2.2.

---

Definitions 2.2, 2.3, and 2.4 define three major subsets of the basic character set as given in 2.1. Some special considerations and connotations for certain characters are presented next.

2.4 Special Characters

+ — * / = . & ( ) , ' and the *blank*

A subset of the basic character set, different from either 2.2 or 2.3.

2.5 Alphanumeric or Alphameric Characters

**ABCDEFGHIJKLMNOPQRSTUVWXYZ$0123456789**

A subset of the basic character set comprised of the two subsets, alphabetic and numeric, as defined in 2.2 and 2.3.

2.6 Mathematical Operators

**+ — * /**

+ means addition, — means subtraction, * means multiplication, / means division, and ** means exponentiation. All four characters form a subset of the special character set, as given in 2.4.

2.7 Assignment Operator

=

The = sign means "to be replaced by," not "equal to" as is normal in algebra. It is also a member of the special character set, as given in 2.4.

2.8 Decimal Point

The decimal point is used only as a decimal point and nothing else. It is also a member of the special character set, as given in 2.4.

2.9 The Punctuation Characters

, ( ) '

These characters are used to separate or delimit other elements in the language to be defined later. They also form a subset of the special character set, as given in 2.4.

---

2.10 Delimiters

---

. , ( ) = + − * / ' &

---

Special characters, excluding the blank, which separate more complex elements of the language.

---

## 2.3 *WORDS* OF THE LANGUAGE

A plateau in the complexity of the language has now been reached. In English, this level would be the point where words are formed from letters. All acceptable English words and their meanings are given in a dictionary. Fortran IV is different, in that rules for forming *words* are provided the user, but without a dictionary. Meanings attributed to the words, therefore, must be arbitrary and are completely up to the programmer.

The rules for this level, the word level, are presented now. Following each rule several examples are given along with further discussion.

---

2.11 Constants

---

A sequence of digits among which may appear a decimal point, + or − sign, or the letter **E**.

---

A quantity that does not change during the course of computation.

---

**Examples:**

> 372013
> 2.9638
> −30.27
> 1.6E−6
> 7.5E+8

Almost all problems that are suitable for solution on a computer involve constants at some point during the computational process. For example, in computations involving the circle and its components such as the radius, diameter, or area, the value of pi (3.1415 . . . ) may appear, or the quantity 2, as in the relation between the radius and the diameter of a circle (D = 2R). All values such as these never change. Whenever the programmer needs to include such a quantity in the procedure to solve a problem, he merely writes it into his program. There are several types of constants or quantities, which are used in Fortran IV. Two types are presented and discussed now. Others will be discussed in Chapter 7.

---

2.12 Integer Mode Constant (Obsolete Term: Fixed Point)

A sequence of digits, optionally preceded by + or −. No decimal point may be included.

A quantity that is always a whole number, valued between −2147483648 and +2147483647.

---

**Examples:**

> 3764
> 3
> 0
> − 3295
> + 10773

The major characteristic of integer constants is the absence of the decimal point. Therefore, it is guaranteed that the value will always be an integer. Integer values are provided for in Fortran IV primarily for counting purposes, however they may be used in many computations.

The limits placed on the range of integer numbers are dictated by the computer's storage word size. The IBM System/360 has a word size of 32 binary bits, thus the largest positive number allowed is $2^{31} - 1$ or 2,147,483,647. Because of the way numbers are maintained, the absolute value of the largest negative value is one greater than the positive maximum, therefore the lower limit on integers is $-2,147,483,648$.

---

2.13 Real Mode Constant (Obsolete Term: Floating Point)

---

A sequence of digits containing a decimal point, optionally preceeded by a + or − sign, and also optionally followed by a letter **E**, a sign and an exponent if using scientific notation.

---

A quantity that may be fractional or mixed with a range of approximately $\pm 10^{-75}$ to $\pm 10^{75}$.

---

**Examples:**

```
3.5
− 15.89
3.0E + 6        equivalent to 3.0 x 10⁶ or 3000000.0
2.7E − 4        equivalent to 2.7 x 10⁻⁴ or 0.00027
0.0
− 7.2E − 35     equivalent to − 7.2 x 10⁻³⁵
```

The major differentiating characteristic of real constants is the presence of the decimal point. This character allows the quantity to have a fraction part. If the quantity has a zero fraction, then the value is integer. However, it is stored and operated upon by the computer in a way different from the integer constant written without a decimal point.

Again the limits on the range of the real numbers is a peculiarity of the computer being used. A more exact set of limitations for the IBM System/360 is:

largest magnitude number is $7.2 \times 10^{75}$
smallest magnitude number is $2.4 \times 10^{-78}$

Thus the total range of real numbers includes:

$$-7.2 \times 10^{75} \text{ to } -2.4 \times 10^{-78}, 0.0,$$
$$2.4 \times 10^{-78} \text{ to } 7.2 \times 10^{75}.$$

Quantities expressed by real numbers in the computer usually have approximately seven to eight places of accuracy. In other words, the power of ten, or the exponent, has no direct effect on the accuracy of the magnitude of the number, as the magnitude and the exponent are maintained separately by the computer.

On the same level of the language as constants are symbols, variables, and functions.

---

2.14 Symbol

---

A sequence of 1 to 6 alphanumeric characters (letters and/or digits) the first of which must be a letter.

---

Symbols will be used as variable, function, and subroutine names.

**Examples:**

X
ALPHA
DATA
SQRT
X5
ITEM63
$3
$AB

---

2.15  Variable

---

Same as symbol, given in Definition 2.14.

---

Symbolizes, represents, or names a quantity which may vary during the course of computation.

---

**Examples:**

RADIUS
XYZ
A12
BETA
E
ITEM

Just as constants are provided to represent quantities that do not change during computation, provision must be made for quantities that do change. It should be clear that in order to refer to a changing quantity we must give it a name. But it should be understood that the characters in the variable name, with one exception, have no direct effect on the value which the name represents. For example, the variable name

A12 does not mean its value is twelve. The one exception mentioned is the first letter of the variable. This letter determines the mode of the quantity represented, such as integer or real.

---

2.16 Integer Mode Variable

First letter must be either **I, J, K, L, M,** or **N.**

Quantity represented must lie between −2147483648 and 2147483647.

---

**Examples:**

    J
    K5
    IXYZ
    LINE
    MATRIX

Integer variables correspond to integer constants in that the quantities represented by integer variables are subject to the same limitations placed on integer constants. The computer treats integer constants and the quantities represented by integer variables in precisely the same way.

---

2.17 Real Mode Variable

First letter must not be **I, J, K, L, M,** or **N.**

Quantity represented must lie between approximately $\pm 10^{-75}$ and $\pm 10^{+75}$.

---

**Examples:**

X
GAMMA
A5
DATA2
$$7
A$

The same remarks apply to the relationship between real constants and the quantities represented by real variables as they do for integer quantities. Other types of variables will be discussed in Chapter 7.

| 2.18 Function Names |
| --- |
| Same as symbols, as given in Definition 2.14. |
| Represent specific computational procedures which are used often enough to justify providing separate programs for their solution. |

Methods of defining functions will be discussed in Chapter 6. For the present, only system-supplied functions are presented and only a small portion of those available is discussed. See Appendix 1 for a complete list of supplied functions.

Provisions are made in Fortran IV to obtain access to prewritten programs to solve certain often encountered problems, such as finding the square root of a quantity. A rule in the next section shows how the function names are used to perform the desired operations.

---

2.19 System-Supplied Functions

---

Specifically reserved symbols such as **SQRT, ALOG, ALOG10, SIN, COS, ATAN, EXP,** and **ABS.**

---

Represent respectively the specific computational procedures for the square root, log to the base *e*, log to the base 10, the trigonometric sine, cosine, and arctangent, exponentiation to the base *e*, and finally the absolute value.

---

## 2.4 THE *PHRASES* OF THE LANGUAGE

Another level has now been reached in the Fortran IV language complexity. This new level can be compared with the phrase level of English, between the word and sentence levels. In Fortran IV, *phrases* are referred to as expressions.

---

2.20 Expression

---

Any valid combination of constants, variables, or functions separated by the math operators or punctuation characters, as defined in 2.21 through 2.26. This combination may include the single occurrence of a constant, variable, or function implementation.

---

Represents a mathematical thought.

**Examples:**
    3.5
    X
    X + Y
    SQRT(X)

The above definition for expression is very general. To provide a more precise definition, six basic rules are stated. These rules can be used to derive any valid expression or to determine the acceptability of any existing sequence of characters as an expression. Discussion follows Rule 6.

---

2.21 Rule 1 for Expressions

---

Any constant or variable is an expression.

---

**Examples:**
    ALPHA
    − 3.2
    X10

---

2.22 Rule 2 for Expressions

---

If **E** is an expression, and if its first character is not + or −, then +**E** and −**E** are expressions.

---

**Examples:**
    −X
    +2.5
    −10

---

2.23 Rule 3 for Expressions

---

If **E** is an expression, then **(E), ((E))**, and so on, are expressions.

---

**Examples:**
(X)
(+X)
(−3.5)

---

2.24 Rule 4 for Expressions

---

If **SMFUN** is the name of <u>some</u> <u>func</u>tion of *n* variables, and if **E**, **F**, . . . , **H** are a set of *n* expressions, then **SMFUN (E, F, . . . , H)** is an expression.

---

**Examples:**
SQRT(X)
SQRT(−Y)
ALOG(GAMMA)

---

2.25 Rule 5 for Expressions

---

If **E** and **F** are expressions, and if the first character of **F** is not + or −, then **E + F, E − F, E * F**, and **E/F** are expressions.

**Examples:**

X + Y
A / BETA
A + Y − Z
A * (B − C)

---

2.26 Rule 6 for Expressions

---

If **E** and **F** are expressions, and if the first character of **F** is not + or −, then **E ** F** is an expression and means $E^F$ or *E* to the *F* power.

---

**Examples:**

A**5
X**(−B)
(A+B)**3

These rules or definitions for expressions may seem rather strange to some. This uneasiness may be attributed to the phenomenon of *recursion.* Simply stated, recursion means the term being defined can be found in the definition itself. In other words, expressions can be made up of simpler expressions. This behavior is exhibited by all but the first of the six rules.

Rule 1 is the basic rule, indicating that all expressions must be built out of constants or- variables, or both. In addition, constants and variables express mathematical thoughts even though they are trivial cases.

It could also be pointed out that all of the foregoing material on constants, variables, and expressions is not appreciably different from the principles embodied in high-school algebra.

Rule 2 is the definition of the two unary (single-operand) operators, + and −. The + unary operator is redundant and it has no effect on the expression whatever.

The — unary operator inverts the algebraic sign of the expression. The phrase "and if its first character is not + or —" prohibits the appearance of two operators in a row, such as ++ X, +— X, —+ X, or ——X.

Rule 3 has an effect on operator hierarchy, the topic of the next section. Suffice it to say here that there is a major difference between the two following expressions:

$$A * B + C \qquad A * (B + C)$$

Rule 4 sounds very complicated but it merely describes the correct method of writing a function name with its arguments. A function name is a reference to a specific computational procedure, such as the square root, called SQRT. A square root can only be found from a given quantity. This quantity, in general, is called the argument of the function. Also since the square root is a function of only one variable the square root can be derived from only one quantity. Then according to Rule 4 the implementation of the square root would look as follows:

$$SQRT(E)$$

In words, the reserved name SQRT would be written followed by the single argument (any one expression) enclosed in parentheses.

**Examples:**
SQRT(A+B)
ABS(X*Y)

Rule 5 is the definition of the four binary (two operands) operators: + for addition, — for subtraction, * for multiplication, and / for division. Again, "and if the first character of F is not + or —" prohibits two operators occurring side by side. These four operations, of course, are the common mathematical operations with which everyone is familiar.

Rule 6 defines another binary operator, **, an exception to the side-by-side rule, that is called exponentiation. In other words, the first operand is raised to the power of the second operand. Again the ** operator cannot occur beside another operator. For example, if one wanted to raise $X$ to the $-Y$ power, it would be written

$$X**(-Y), \qquad not \qquad X**-Y.$$

As an example of the application of these rules, a familiar expression will be tested for its acceptability in terms of Fortran IV. The expression chosen expresses one of the roots of the quadratic equation $Ax^2 + Bx + C = 0$. The expression in ordinary algebra would look as follows:

$$\frac{-B + \sqrt{B^2 - 4AC}}{2A}$$

In Fortran IV, this can be written

$$(-B + SQRT (B ** 2 - 4 * A * C)) / (2 * A)$$

In Table A, this expression is decomposed into its basic variables and constants, which by Rule 1 are each individual expressions. Then when the appropriate rules are applied, the parts gradually recombine into their original order. The rule number being applied at each particular step is given at the right-hand margin. Please notice that the rule may be applied several times on the same step.

TABLE A

| Step | Expressions | | | | Rule |
|------|-------------|---|---|---|------|
| | (−B+SQRT(B**2−4*A*C))/(2*A) | | | | |
| 1 | B | B  2  4  A  C | 2  A | | 1 |
| 2 | −B | B  2  4  A  C | 2  A | | 2 |
| 3 | −B | B**2  4  A  C | 2  A | | 6 |
| 4 | −B | B**2  4*A  C | 2*A | | 5 |
| 5 | −B | B**2  4*A*C | 2*A | | 5 |
| 6 | −B | B**2−4*A*C | 2*A | | 5 |
| 7 | −B SQRT(B**2−4*A*C) | | 2*A | | 4 |
| 8 | −B+SQRT(B**2−4*A*C) | | 2*A | | 5 |
| 9 | (−B+SQRT(B**2−4*A*C)) | | (2*A) | | 3 |
| 10 | (−B+SQRT(B**2−4*A*C))/(2*A) | | | | 5 |

Therefore, the original sequence of characters is a valid expression in Fortran IV. Even though it appears that some rules could be applied in a different order, they may not. At the same time it may not be clear why the pairs of parentheses are placed around the numerator and the denominator. These questions are answered in Section 2.5 on hierarchy.

## 2.5 EXPRESSION HIERARCHIES

---

2.27 Hierarchy

---

Any system of things in graded order or a series of successive terms of different rank.

---

The concept of hierarchy can be applied to Fortran IV expressions in two different ways. One hierarchy is applied to operators, the other to operands. This places the operators and operands in two individual orders of precedence.

---

2.28 Operator Hierarchy

---

1. Exponentiation.
2. Multiplication or division.
3. Addition or subtraction.

---

Operator hierarchy ranking indicates that the operation of exponentiation is done before any others. Multiplication or division is done next, followed by addition or subtraction.

Several examples may help to clarify the concept of operator hierarchy. Looking at the expression,

$$A + B * C - D$$

without any particular rule of interpretation, the following different interpretations of its meaning could be assumed:

1. (A + B) * (C − D)
2. A + (B * C) − D
3. ((A + B) * C) − D
4. A + (B * (C − D))

Because of the Fortran IV rule of grammar, described by Definition 2.28, the interpretation given in the second choice is the one assumed by the system as proper. If the programmer has in mind one of the other choices, the parentheses must be included to indicate the intended choice.

Perhaps the following example involving division better illustrates the critical effect on results that the order of operator execution can have.

The expression

$$A + B / C + D$$

could be interpreted as

1. (A + B) / (C + D)
2. A + (B / C) + D
3. ((A + B) / C) + D
4. A + (B / (C + D))

Again, Fortran IV is designed to assume the second choice to be the intended one. Notice here the difference between the first and second choice. In the first, A is part of·the numerator of the quotient, while in the second it is not. In the first, D is part of the denominator of the quotient, in the second it is not.

It might be mentioned here that the programmer may insert more parentheses into an expression than are necessary to guarantee the intent of the meaning. Usually, more than enough parentheses cause no harm, while too few can be misleading to the computer. Quite often the programmer unknowingly makes certain assumptions, while the computer, unable to read the user's mind, proceeds on a different course.

Looking at Table A, we can now see why the exponentiation in Step 3 is performed before the multiplication of Step 4. Likewise, why the multiplications of Steps 4 and 5 are done before the subtraction of Step 6. Otherwise, entirely different results are obtained.

Now, it also should be clear why Step 9 is required before Step 10. Otherwise, when the division is performed, the term −B is not included in the numerator, nor is the A included in the denominator of the quotient.

---

**2.29 Mixed Mode Expression**

---

An expression containing operands of both integer and real modes.

---

**2.30 Operand Hierarchy**

---

1. Real mode.
2. Integer mode.

In expressions containing only integer constants or variables, all the indicated operations to be performed by the computer are executed exclusively in integer arithmetic. Likewise, expressions made up entirely of real elements are executed in real arithmetic. However, in expressions containing both integer and real elements, called mixed expressions, a conversion from integer to real is performed by the computer, leaving the final result in the real mode. To maintain as much accuracy as possible, real quantities must take precedence over integer, otherwise extremely large or small numbers, as well as all fraction parts, are truncated and lost.

---

**2.31 Ordering within an Operator Hierarchy Level**

---

1. For addition and subtraction or multiplication and division the ordering is from left to right.
2. For exponentiation, **, the ordering is from right to left.

Within the example,

$$A + B - C + D - E$$

all of the operators, + and −, fall within the same operator hierarchy level, level three, of Definition 2.28. The order of the operations is critical because the subtract operation is not commutative. Fortran IV executes the operations from the left to the right, thus determining the correct order of the operations. The above example is executed as if it were written

$$(((A + B) - C) + D) - E$$

The same rule applies to an expression containing multiplication and division operations, such as:

$$A / B * C / D * E$$

This example is interpreted as:

$$(((A / B) * C) / D) * E$$

However, the exponentiation operation, **, is performed in the opposite direction, or right to left. In other words, the example

$$A ** B ** C ** D$$

is executed as if it were written

$$A ** (B ** (C ** D))$$

## 2.6  STATEMENTS IN FORTRAN IV

The discussion of statements in Fortran IV occurs at the next level of complexity in the language. This level precedes the final step of writing a complete program in Fortran IV.

Statements in Fortran IV can be compared with sentences in English. A Fortran IV program is made up of statements, just as a paragraph of English writing is made up of sentences.

---

**2.32 Fortran IV Statements**

---

Specific combinations of special reserved words (such as **IF, DO, READ**), basic characters, variables, constants, and expressions punched or typed in columns 7–72 of a card or line. Each statement must begin on a separate card or line. Statements may continue on one or more cards or lines by making column 6 of the continuation cards or lines a nonblank.

---

Indicate specific actions to be taken by the computer, such as read data, compute a quantity, and print result.

---

There are approximately thirty specific kinds of Fortran IV statements. They can be grouped into four general categories:

1. Arithmetic statements,
2. Control statements,
3. Input and output statements,
4. Specification statements.

A brief general discussion of each type of statement occurs here; presentation of details will follow in later sections and chapters. A complete summary of all statements will be given in Appendix 2.

The arithmetic statement is used to command the computer to carry out some specific computation. It resembles a formula and contains an expression. Again, this is the origin of the name Fortran.

Control statements are used to convey to the machine commands to carry out operations such as branching, looping, or simply stopping. The power of the computer becomes useful only when the user has the ability to make decisions and perform alternative tasks dependent on the outcome of those decisions. Control statements provide this capability.

Without input or output statements, it is difficult to communicate with a program while it is executing, to input data, or to output results. Input and output statements provide a means for the program to communicate with the outside world during execution.

Specification statements include all of the other statements not classified under the first three categories. In general, they specify information pertinent to the execution of a program, but rarely cause action to be taken during execution. Rephrasing, specification statements are considered to be nonexecutable statements, in contrast with all the others which are executable.

One further remark should be made in reference to Fortran IV statements. Fortran IV can be described as a *narrative* or procedural computer language in the sense that a specific set of steps is specified by a Fortran IV program for the computer to follow in solving a problem.

The step-by-step program is assumed by the computer to proceed from one statement to the next in the order in which they are written. Hence the use of the term narrative. This standard ordering holds true until a control statement is encountered. The computer may then perform a branch or transfer. After the transfer, however, normal sequencing will continue from this new point until another control statement is encountered. Discussion of control statements occurs in Chapter 3.

## 2.7 THE ARITHMETIC STATEMENT

| 2.33 Arithmetic Statement |
|---|
| **A = B,**<br>where **A** is any variable<br>and **B** is any expression. |
| Indicates to the computer to evaluate the expression **B** and to make the variable **A** equal to the result. |

The Fortran IV arithmetic statement probably has the simplest standard form of all the statements. Due to the almost infinite combinations of variables and expressions, however, the appearance of actual arithmetic statements is almost unlimited.

The exact appearance and meaning of a given arithmetic statement is primarily limited only by the programmer's imagination and his treatment of the problem being solved.

The actual behavior of the computer during the execution of an arithmetic statement can best be described by example. Given the example used in Section 4 and Table A, a statement involving a root of the quadratic equation looks as follows:

X = (− B + SQRT (B ** 2 − 4 * A * C)) / (2 * A)

This statement is a command to the computer to compute the value of the expression on the right using the current values of A, B, and C and to make this result the value of X. Implied in this statement are three important facts:

1.  The current values of A, B, and C are provided by other statements appearing before this statement in the sequence being executed by the computer.
2.  The result of the computations indicated by the expression replaces any previous value that X might have had.
3.  Finally, the original value of A, B, and C remain unchanged.

A rule can be formulated for the evaluation or execution of an arithmetic statement.

---

2.34 Rule Concerning Arithmetic Statements

---

The value of the variable on the left of the equal sign generally changes. The values of variables on the right remain unchanged, unless the same variable appears on both sides.

---

For further discussion, simpler examples are useful. The following statement

$$A = B$$

is probably the simplest. It causes the value of A to be made the same as that of B. The value of B remains unchanged. The value of A changes unless it equals B before the computer reaches this statement.

The statements

$$X = I \quad \text{or} \quad I = X$$

illustrate something more than just a replacement of one value by another. An apparent change in mode is being specified. Occasionally this change is a very useful operation.

An interesting point is made by the following example:

$$I = I + 1$$

This statement graphically illustrates the meaning of the equal sign in Fortran IV, which is to replace the value of the left-hand side by the value of the right. It should be obvious that the above statement does not satisfy the normally accepted, algebraic meaning of the equal sign. The above statement in Fortran IV causes the current value of I to be increased by 1, changing the value of a variable on both sides of the equal sign. There is no violation of Rule 2.34. (The degenerate case of A = A does violate the Rule given in 2.34.)

We return now to the more difficult statement:

X = (− B + SQRT (B ** 2 − 4 * A * C)) / (2 * A)

This statement computes one of the roots to the quadratic equation. To obtain the second root, we must write a separate statement. However, the two roots need to be uniquely identified, thus two different variable names must be created. So, to compute both roots, the following two statements may be written:

X1 = (− B + SQRT (B ** 2 − 4 * A * C)) / (2 * A)
X2 = (− B − SQRT (B ** 2 − 4 * A * C)) / (2 * A)

The sequence of computer operations commanded by these two statements is the following:

1. The right side of the first statement is evaluated using the current values of A, B, and C.
2. The value of X1 is made equal to the result of Step 1.
3. The right-hand side of the second statement is evaluated using the same values of A, B, and C. They were unchanged by Steps 1 and 2.
4. The value of X2 is made equal to the result of Step 3.

This chapter concludes by illustrating two additional points concerning arithmetic statements. The first, a matter of continuity in variable value, is fairly important for beginners to understand. The second, a matter of program efficiency, is not so important to the beginner; however, an early appreciation of practical efficiency is of long-term value to the prospective programmer. Both points can be illustrated with the same example.

By looking closely at the two statements above for X1 and X2, we see that a great many of the indicated computer operations are repetitious and time-consuming. The following set of six statements produces the same results in about half the time.

```
DIV = 2 * A
RAD = B ** 2 − 4 * A * C
TERM1 = − B / DIV
TERM2 = SQRT (RAD) / DIV
X1 = TERM1 + TERM2
X2 = TERM1 − TERM2
```

As for continuity of the variable value, it should be noted that once DIV has been computed by the first statement, that quantity remains unchanged until DIV again appears on the left-hand side of the equal sign. Until that time, the value is available for computation in the evaluation of the right-hand side of later statements, such as the third and fourth statements. By the same token, RAD computed by the second statement can be used in the fourth statement. TERM1 computed by the third and TERM2 computed by the fourth can be used in the fifth and sixth statements. This concept of continuity holds true throughout the Fortran IV language and within a given Fortran IV program.

The final evidence of machine time saved can be illustrated by adding up the different types of operations in the two methods and comparing the results.

| *Operation* | *Two-statement method* | *Six-statement method* |
|-------------|:----------------------:|:----------------------:|
| Addition | 1 | 1 |
| Subtraction | 5 | 3 |
| Multiplication | 6 | 3 |
| Division | 2 | 2 |
| Exponentiation | 2 | 1 |
| SQRT | 2 | 1 |
| equal signs | 2 | 6 |

Note that subtractions were almost halved; multiplications, exponentiations, and square roots were halved. The only increase was in equal signs, an operation requiring a relatively small amount of computer time. The operations accounting for a large portion of the time are the exponentiations and the square roots, both of which were halved. Thus it is true that the six-statement method is more efficient than the two-statement method.

Of course, compilation may require slightly more time with the six-statement method than with the two-statement approach. However, it should be remembered that a program is meant to be executed many times, while compilation is usually done only once.

## PRACTICE EXERCISES

2.1 Most of the characters in the basic character set, Definition 2.1, can individually satisfy a number of other definitions within Chapter 2. For each of the basic characters, indicate all, if any, of the other definitions which are also satisfied.

2.2 Using the numbers 1 through 10 to identify Definitions 2.1 through 2.10 and their corresponding sets, indicate all those sets in which each of the following groups of characters belong (some may belong to several sets). For example, *) would be sets 1 and 10.

|  |  |  |  |
|---|---|---|---|
| (a) | $ABCDE | (f) | + − * / |
| (b) | 0123 | (g) | = |
| (c) | . | (h) | & ( ) − |
| (d) | + , ( ' | (i) | ( , ' ) |
| (e) | XYZ01$ | (j) | A − 3 |

2.3 All of the following are illegal integer mode constants or variables. Why?

|  |  |  |  |
|---|---|---|---|
| (a) | MBCDXYZ | (f) | − 2.5 |
| (b) | SA | (g) | M − A |
| (c) | A5 | (h) | 0.5 |
| (d) | M5. | (i) | *IJK |
| (e) | 25654689910 | (j) | XYZ |

2.4 All of the following are illegal real mode constants or variables. Why?

|  |  |  |  |
|---|---|---|---|
| (a) | 3769 | (f) | E + 8 |
| (b) | − 17 | (g) | 1.3E + 123 |
| (c) | $$$$$$$$ | (h) | 3.5X |
| (d) | K7 | (i) | SQRT (X) |
| (e) | − IJK | (j) | IREAL |

2.5 Associate each element in list A (Fortran element) with an element from list B (English element).

|      List A      |   List B   |
|:---------------:|:---------:|
|                 |           |

Control statement     Letter
Real mode constant     Word
Expression     Phrase
Real mode variable     Sentence
Symbol
Digit
Plus sign
Integer mode constant
Function name
Variable
Arithmetic statement
Integer mode variable

2.6 Construct tables similar to Table A and determine the validity of the following expressions.

(a) 3.4*SQRT(−B/C+ALOG(ALPHA))/A**(2*B)

(b) A ** SIN (B + C) / D − E * A / (F / C − D)

2.7 By adding more parentheses to the expressions in Exercise 2.6, show the order of the various operations.

2.8 Given the following sequence of statements, indicate the result of each.

X = 3.5
I = 4
K = I + X
Y = I + X
J = K + Y
I = I + 2.5
X = X + Y

2.9 Given:

AI=EXP(R*X)*COS(S*X)+EXP(−R*X)*SIN(S*X)

A2=EXP(R*X)*COS(S*X)−EXP(−R*X)*SIN(S*X)

Show a more efficient sequence of statements yielding the same results.

2.10 Match each element on the left with as many elements on the right as are applicable.

(a) + 37                         Symbol
(b) (15.6)                       Integer constant
(c) A = A + 1                    Real constant
(d) ROW                         Integer variable
(e) − 4.321E + 60               Real variable
(f) X + 3.2E + 60               Expression
(g) XYZ = KLA + 2               Statement
(h) LINE
(i) 34725
(j) − A

2.11 Indicate the numeric result of each of the following statements:

ANS1 = 1 + 2/5
ANS2 = 1 + 5/2
ANS3 = 1 + 2./5
ANS4 = 1 + 5./2
ANS5 = 1 + 5./2.5
ANS6 = (1 + 5.) / 2.5

2.12 What is the value of A in the following program:

ADJ = 6.54
HYP = 3.27
RATIO = ADJ / HYP
RATIO = RATIO + 2
A = SQRT (RATIO)

CHAPTER **3**

# Decision,
# Branching, and
# Control Operations

## 3.1 INTRODUCTION

This chapter will be concerned primarily with control statements with the exception of the DO statement, which will be discussed in Chapter 5. The concept of flow charting, also introduced here, is a pictorial representation of a program which allows visual inspection in a different form. However, it is the opinion of this author that in most cases, the drawing of a flow chart essentially means writing a program twice. This duplicity between a pictorial diagram and its Fortran statement counterpart is illustrated throughout this chapter. It is further felt that most prospective programmers can be trained to program without the necessity of drawing flow charts except for very difficult problems. Once the implied logic of a statement is understood, the programmer should be able to put most programs together mentally without the need for drawing a diagram.

## 3.2  FLOW CHARTING ARITHMETIC STATEMENTS

As a simple example of a flow chart, Figure 3.1 is a representation of the last program example in Chapter 2. The program contains six arithmetic statements.

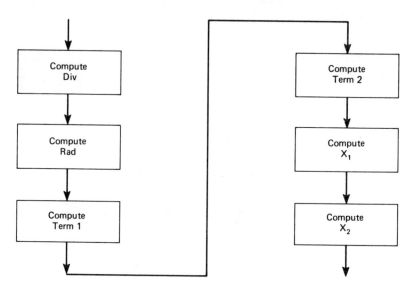

**Figure 3.1  A flow chart.**

This is merely a restatement of the program in a different form. However, to the beginner the sequence of operations may be more obvious in this diagram than in the original program segment. After computing the value of DIV, the natural sequence is to go forward to the next block or statement and to compute RAD. The point to be made is that this same natural sequence is seen in the original presentation of the program in Fortran arithmetic statements. The equivalence between the two presentations is shown in Figure 3.2.

An obvious step can be taken here to simplify the diagram in Figure 3.1. All of the indicated computations could be implied by one box, as in Figure 3.3.

This technique is used in actual practice to de-emphasize such simple natural sequences in the flow chart, allowing the more complicated sequences within a program to stand out.

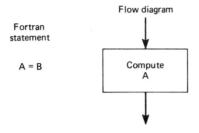

**Figure 3.2 Flow chart equivalence.**

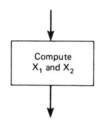

**Figure 3.3 Simplified flow chart.**

## 3.3 CONTROL STATEMENTS IN GENERAL

Occasionally, the natural sequence of statement execution must be altered in some fashion. In fact, without some means of altering this natural sequence, automatic computers would be almost useless. This need becomes more and more obvious as one becomes familiar with computers and how they operate.

Basically, there are only a few ways of altering the natural sequence of program execution. These might be listed as follows:

1. Stopping at a point,
2. Jumping from one point to another
   a. Unconditionally,
   b. Conditionally,
3. Repeating or looping through a segment.

Actually, these three methods are considered special cases of the single operation of jumping or branching from one point in a program to another.

The first variation, that of stopping, in most cases is not a complete stop, but rather a jump or branch from within a user's program back to the monitor program. This return allows a sequence of jobs to be performed on the computer with a minimum of idle time between each job, as discussed in Chapter 1.

The third variation, that of looping or repeating a program segment, is jumping or branching more than once from one point in a program to another. There is only one complication here. How does the computer determine when to stop looping?

Control statements in their several different forms provide the necessary program ingredient for specifying any of these variations on the theme, "branch or branch not." Before discussing the use of control statements in detail, the subject of statement numbers must first be considered.

---

3.1 Statement Number

---

One to five digits typed or punched in columns 1 to 5 of the line or card.

---

Provides a reference point for other statements.

---

Each statement within a program may be given a statement number. Statements need not be numbered unless referred to either by control statements or some other statement. No two statement numbers within a program may be the same. In other words, all statement numbers within a program must be unique. Additionally, these statement numbers may be in any numerical sequence. Statement number sequence has no direct effect on the program sequence or the order in which statements will be executed. Normal sequence is still that presented in previous sections.

Therefore, statement numbers serve only as reference points so that other statements may refer to particular points within the program.

## 3.4 LINE OR CARD FORMAT

The physical layout or format of statements and statement numbers within lines of a Fortran IV program must conform to certain requirements. Each line contains three segments or fields as shown in Figure 3.4.

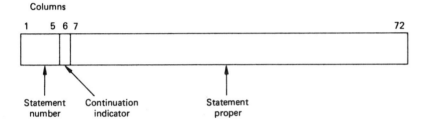

**Figure 3.4  Fortran IV statement format.**

The three fields making up a line are:

1. Columns 1 through 5 contain the statement number, if one has been given to the statement.
2. Column 6 is always blank for the beginning of a new statement. A nonblank (also nonzero) in column 6 indicates that this line is a continuation of the previous line.
3. Columns 7 through 72 contain the Fortran IV statement. A specific example appears in Figure 3.5.

Columns

| 1 | 5 6 7 | | 72 |
|---|---|---|---|
| 27 | | X1 = Term 1 + Term 2 | |

**Figure 3.5  Fortran IV statement example.**

Here the statement number is 27. Since this is the beginning of a new statement, column 6 is blank. The statement is an arithmetic statement as formerly discussed and it may appear anywhere within columns 7 through 72.

A letter C in column 1 designates the entire line or card as a comments card or line which has no effect on the program.

Program statements, program segments, and programs henceforth will be presented in this standard format. Wherever it is desirable to indicate branching, the program sequence will be shown by arrows outside the left margin of the statement number field. When no arrows appear, as in arithmetic statements, the normal sequence from one statement to the next is implied.

Also, when a new type of statement is being discussed, a general presentation will be given with the statement embedded within a general program segment. Statements above and below the statement under discussion will be represented by blank lines, as seen in Section 3.5.

## 3.5 THE UNCONDITIONAL BRANCHING STATEMENT

When a simple unconditional branch or transfer is made from one program point to another, the following statement may be used.

---

3.2 Unconditional Transfer Statement

---

GO TO *N*,
where *N* is a statement number of an executable statement.

---

Indicates that normal sequencing is to be interrupted by a jump or transfer to the statement whose number is *N*.

---

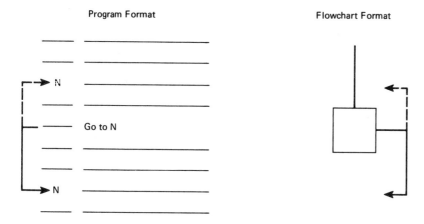

**Figure 3.6** GO TO *N* **standard form.**

The presentation, in Figure 3.6, of the unconditional transfer statement, GO TO *N*, indicates that upon reaching the GO TO *N* statement, the computer interrupts normal sequencing. Control transfers either forward (solid line) or backward (dashed line) depending on whether the statement numbered *N* is physically below or above the GO TO *N*.

A specific example is shown in Firgure 3.7. Here, the statement whose number is 36 is below the GO TO 36 statement. Therefore, the transfer is forward to statement 36, skipping all statements in between. To insure proper operation of the compiler, a statement number must be given

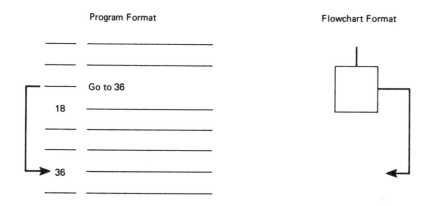

**Figure 3.7** GO TO *N* **example.**

to the first statement after the GO TO, as shown, otherwise a portion of the program could never be reached.

It should be obvious that if the GO TO $N$ statement refers to the very next statement in sequence, as GO TO 18 would in Figure 3.7, the sequence reverts to normal sequencing, thus the GO TO statement may be left out completely.

Nothing but trouble is gained by using a GO TO $N$ statement whose own statement number is $N$. If the compiler or interpreter does not check for such possibilities, a program containing such a statement gets caught in a loop for an indefinite time.

## 3.6 THE CONDITIONAL TRANSFER STATEMENTS

The first conditional transfer statement discussed is the IF statement.

---

3.3 Conditional Transfer Statement (IF)

---

**IF** *(E)* $N_1, N_2, N_3,$
where $E$ is any expression and the $N_i$ are statement numbers of executable statements.

---

Indicates normal sequencing is to be interrupted by a jump to $N_1$ if the value of $E$ is less than zero, to $N_2$ if $E$ equals zero, or to $N_3$ if $E$ is greater than zero.

---

Figure 3.8 illustrates the general behavior of the IF statement.

There are three possible branch paths, any one of which can go forward or backward independently.

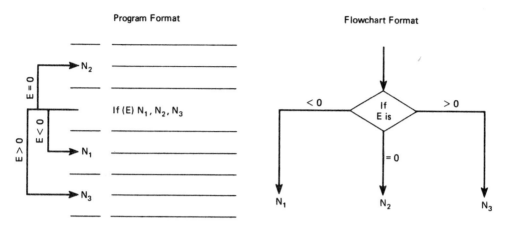

**Figure 3.8** IF **standard form.**

Figure 3.9 illustrates the following IF statement:

$$IF\ (X - 3.5)\ 3,\ 4,\ 5$$

This example also illustrates how the break or decision point for the IF can be moved from zero and placed at a different point, in this case +3.5. This point is illustrated in Figure 3.10.

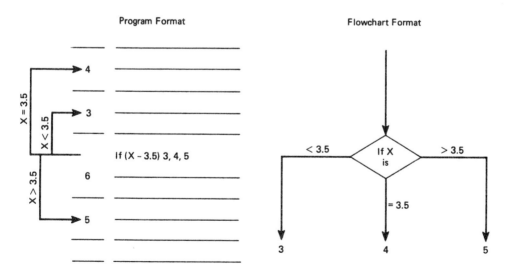

**Figure 3.9** IF **example.**

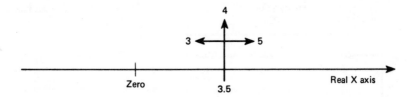

**Figure 3.10 Breakpoint illustration.**

There is no requirement for making all three branch paths different in the IF statement. If two of the three possible conditions lead to the same point, a case as shown in Figure 3.11 is a possible result. Here the second and third branch points are the same. One path is for the "less than" case, while the other path becomes the "greater than" or "equal to" case.

If all three branch points are made the same, as in IF(X) 6, 6, 6, an unconditional branch is specified, therefore the GO TO *N* form accomplishes the same thing.

None of the branch points (statement numbers) specified by the IF may be the same as the IF statement number. Otherwise another endless loop might result. Most compilers, however prohibit such an operation if it is attempted. The first statement after the IF must have a statement number.

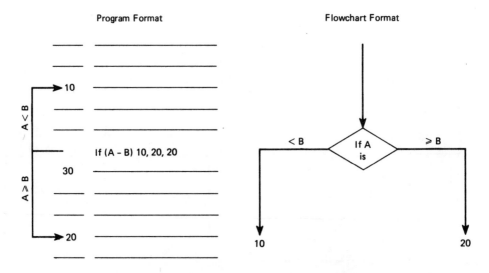

**Figure 3.11 Another IF example.**

To provide a real-life example of how the IF statement works, the final example in Chapter 2 is explored. There, a program segment is presented to compute the roots of the quadratic equation, $Ax^2 + Bx + C = 0$. The given program segment works correctly, provided the value of $B^2 - 4AC$ is not negative. When this quantity is negative, the roots become imaginary and the statement involving the square root of $B^2 - 4AC$ causes an error condition within the computer. Computers cannot obtain the square root of a negative number. Thus something special must be done about this negative condition. Figure 3.12 indicates one way of solving this problem.

An IF statement is inserted into the program segment to test the value of RAD, or $B^2 - 4AC$. If RAD is zero or positive, control proceeds to the statement numbered 1 to execute the same statements as in Chapter 2. As required for real roots, two statements are added to set the imaginary parts to zero. Then transfer is made to the statement numbered 3 to continue the program.

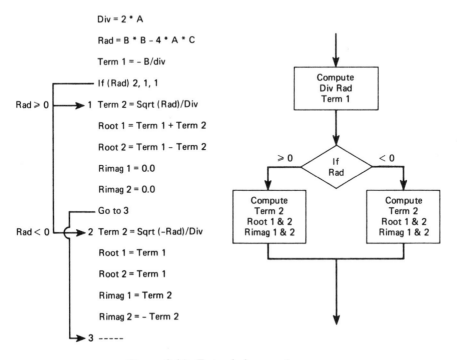

Div = 2 * A

Rad = B * B - 4 * A * C

Term 1 = - B/div

If (Rad) 2, 1, 1

Rad ⩾ 0 → 1 Term 2 = Sqrt (Rad)/Div

Root 1 = Term 1 + Term 2

Root 2 = Term 1 - Term 2

Rimag 1 = 0.0

Rimag 2 = 0.0

Go to 3

Rad < 0 → 2 Term 2 = Sqrt (-Rad)/Div

Root 1 = Term 1

Root 2 = Term 1

Rimag 1 = Term 2

Rimag 2 = - Term 2

3 -----

**Figure 3.12 Extended example.**

If the value of RAD turns up negative, the IF statement causes a transfer to the statement numbered 2. A new sequence of arithmetic statements computes the real and imaginary parts of the roots for this condition.

A second type of conditional transfer statement is called the "computed GO TO."

---

### 3.4 Conditional Transfer Statement (Computed GO TO)

---

GO TO $(N_1, N_2, \ldots, N_m)$, M
where $N_i$ are statement numbers of executable statements and M is any integer variable.

---

Indicates normal sequencing is to be interrupted by a jump to the statement whose number is $N_i$, where $i$ is given by the current value of **M**. If **M** is less than 1 or greater than $m$, then usually normal sequencing will occur.

---

The general description of the computed GO TO statement is shown is Figure 3.13.

In general, any number of statement numbers can be listed in the computed GO TO statement. Of course, if only one number is listed, the GO TO $N$ form is sufficient. Also, for each statement number listed there should be an executable statement somewhere in the program with the same number.

A specific example of a computed GO TO statement is given in Figure 3.14.

As in the IF statement, two or more of the statement numbers in the list of the computed GO TO may be the same, causing a branch to the same point on different values of the integer variable, M.

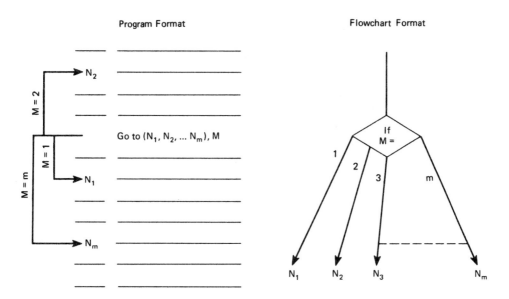

**Figure 3.13  Computed GO TO standard form.**

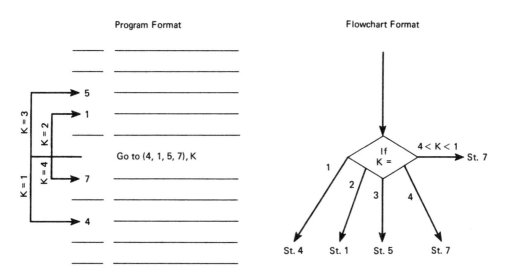

**Figure 3.14  Computed GO TO example.**

For more complete examples of the above concepts, refer to Figures 3.15a and 3.15b. In this program, letter grades are assigned to students depending on their numeric grades, represented by the variable, ISCORE. Letter grades are assigned according to the following scale:

| | |
|---|---|
| Below 60 | E |
| 60 - 69 | D |
| 70 - 79 | C |
| 80 - 89 | B |
| 90 - 100 | A |

In Figures 3.15a and 3.15b the assumption is made that a student's numeric grade is between 0 and 100 and the grade

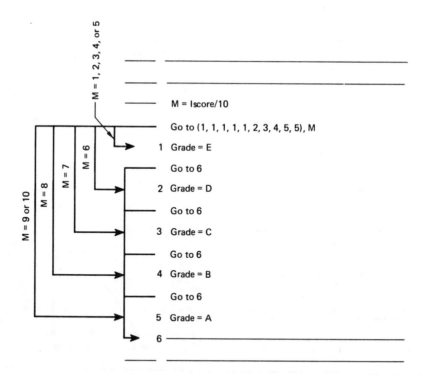

**Figure 3.15a Extended example.**

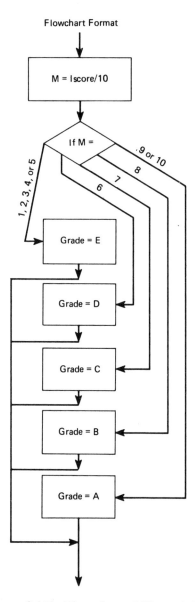

Figure 3.15b Flow chart of Figure 3.15a.

is stored under the variable name ISCORE. The first statement in the program segment computes a value, M, by dividing ISCORE by 10. Since all manipulations here are done in the integer mode, the resulting value of M is an integer with values between 0 and 10.

The computed GO TO statement then sends control to one of 5 statements according to the following scheme:

| *IF* M = | *Control is sent to Statement number* |
|----------|---------------------------------------|
| 0, 1, 2, 3, 4, or 5 | 1 |
| 6 | 2 |
| 7 | 3 |
| 8 | 4 |
| 9 or 10 | 5 |

Thus a letter grade is assigned to the variable, GRADE, according to the desired scale. The exact method of manipulating alphabetic data will be discussed in Chapter 4. Following each grade-assigning statement, control is sent by GO TO *N* type statements to a common point in the program, statement numbered 6. Also notice that a GO TO 6 is not needed after the GRADE = A statement. Normal sequencing is sufficient to arrive at statement 6.

The equivalence between the program format and the flow chart format should now be obvious. If one can picture the behavior depicted by the flow chart by simply looking at the program, there is no need to draw the chart.

The third and final conditional transfer statement is referred to as the "assigned GO TO" statement.

---

3.5 Conditional Transfer Statement (Assigned GO TO)

---

GO TO  M, ($N_1$, $N_2$, . . . , $N_m$)

where **M** is any integer variable used previously in an ASSIGN statement (see Definition 3.6) and $N_i$ are all statement numbers of executable statements.

---

Indicates normal sequencing is to be interrupted by a jump to the statement whose number (from among $N_i$) is equal to the value of **M**. If **M** is not among $N_i$, most compilers will cause transfer to **M** anyway, as **M** must be a valid statement number in order for the program to compile in the first place.

In order to understand the assigned GO TO statement, the ASSIGN statement should be discussed in parallel.

---

3.6 The ASSIGN Statement

---

**ASSIGN *N* TO M**
where ***N*** is an existing statement number of an executable statement and **M** is any integer variable to be used in an assigned GO TO statement.

---

Prepares **M** for use in an assigned GO TO statement to be executed later.

---

It should be apparent from Definitions 3.5 and 3.6, that an ASSIGN statement must be executed before an assigned GO TO statement. This does not mean the former must always appear physically ahead of the latter, only that the former be executed logically before the latter.

The assigned GO TO is similar in appearance to the computed GO TO except for what M represents. In the computed GO TO, M indicates the subscript or position of the statement number in the list. In the assigned GO TO, M indicates the actual statement number to which transfer is to be made. Figure 3.16 shows the general behavior of the assigned GO TO statement.

The behavior indicated in Figure 3.16 is similar to the behavior of the unconditional GO TO. That is, when the statement whose number is $N$ is above the assigned GO TO statement, the transfer is backward, shown with the dashed line. When the statement whose number is $N$ is below the assigned GO TO statement, the transfer is forward, shown with the solid line. The only difference is that the value of the statement number $N$ can change through the use of the ASSIGN statement. Also the possible statement numbers must be taken from the list written in the assigned GO TO statement.

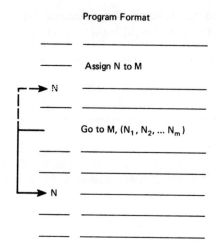

Program Format

Assign N to M

N

Go to M, $(N_1, N_2, ... N_m)$

N

**Figure 3.16** Assigned GO TO standard form.

## 3.7 THE STOP AND END STATEMENTS

In conclusion, this chapter presents a discussion of the STOP and END statements, even though the END is not, strictly speaking, a control statement. Because student programmers usually confuse the meaning of the two statements, an attempt is made to clearly distinguish the meaning and purpose of each in a single presentation. First, the definitions of each:

---

3.7 The STOP Statement

---

**STOP** $n$
where $n$ is an optional number between 1 and 99999.

---

Terminates execution of a program. If included, $n$ is printed on output indicating which STOP terminated the program.

---

3.8 The END statement

---

**END**
Must appear as the final statement of a program.

---

Terminates compilation of a program, if a compiler is used. Usually suspends interpretation of a program, if an interpreter is used.

---

To clearly understand the peculiarities of the STOP and END statements, bear in mind the distinction between the compilation phase and execution phase of a Fortran job, discussed in Chapter 1.

The STOP statement may appear anywhere within a Fortran program, while the END statement must be the final or last statement of a program. The STOP statement can be thought of as representing the logical end of a program and that point where the programmer wishes to terminate execution. This does not have to be at the physical end of the program, nor must it be limited to one occurrence. Several STOP statements may appear throughout a program.

On the other hand, the END statement represents the physical end of a program and that point where the programmer completes the program. Unlike the STOP statement, only one END statement may appear in one program.

As will be seen in Chapter 6, several programs or subprograms may be submitted to the computer in one job. The END statements at the end of each program serve to separate each program from the others.

Another distinction between the two statements is that the STOP statement is executable, while the END is not executable. In other words, an attempt to execute the END should not be made by either transferring to it or arriving at it by natural sequence.

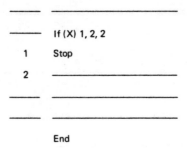

**Figure 3.17** STOP **example.**

Figure 3.17 shows a program segment with the STOP statement appearing in the middle of the program. Its purpose here is to terminate execution if the value of X becomes negative. Other STOP statements could appear elsewhere within the program in addition to the required END at the bottom of the program.

Figure 3.18 shows what usually appears at the very end of a program.

One further point should be made regarding the STOP statement. In most large computer systems, the STOP does not actually stop the computer as it does in some small systems. Instead, control is regained by a supervisor or monitor program outside the user's program. This supervisor program then surveys the job queue to determine which job to run next and proceeds to place this new job into operation. This technique is discussed generally in Chapter 1. In some systems, the user is expected to use a CALL EXIT statement instead of the STOP. However, the result is the same, servicing the next job with a minimum loss of machine time.

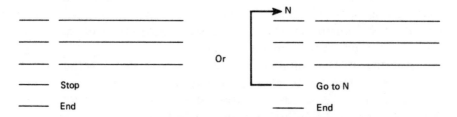

**Figure 3.18 Ending a program.**

An alternative technique for stopping a program, other than using the STOP statement, will be discussed in Chapter 4. There a program will be illustrated that contains no STOP statements. The program is designed to run indefinitely until all available input data is exhausted or is completely processed.

Another alternative is to unplug the machine.

## PRACTICE EXERCISES

3.1 How many ways can the natural sequence of execution of Fortran IV statements be altered?

3.2 What are statement numbers good for?

3.3 True or false:
   (a) The sequence by which program statements are numbered is the sequence by which the program is executed.
   (b) The STOP statement is an executable statement which terminates execution of a program.
   (c) A user may include several END statements in a program, but may use only one STOP statement in a single program.
   (d) The statement number field, the continuation indicator, and the field for the statement are the three fields that make up a line of a Fortran IV program.
   (e) The GO TO $N$ statement is the only statement that can cause an unconditional branch.
   (f) The branching behavior of the IF statement depends on the value of a valid arithmetic expression.
   (g) The integer variable in the computed GO TO and assigned GO TO play the same role.

3.4 How many different branching combinations can be produced with an IF statement?

3.5 Consider the following program segment:

```
        IF (X) 1, 2, 3
1       IF (Y) 4, 5, 6
4       K = 1
        GO TO 7
5       K = 2
        GO TO 7
6       K = 3
        GO TO 7
2       Y = 0.0
        GO TO 1
3       Y = 1.0
        GO TO 1
7       STOP
```

If X and Y have the following values, what is the corresponding value of K? Do X or Y change?

| X | Y | K |
|---|---|---|
| − 5.0 | − 5.0 | |
| − 5.0 | 0.0 | |
| − 5.0 | 5.0 | |
| 0.0 | 4.0 | |
| 5.0 | 1.0 | |

3.6 Write a program segment that reverses the signs of X and Y if both are negative.

3.7 Write the IF statement that places the conditional break point at 7.5 on the $A + B$ axis ($X$ axis with $X = A + B$).

3.8 Why is the IF statement in Figure 3.12 not a three-way branch?

3.9 Assume a tax is zero if earnings are less than $2500.00, 2 percent of amount over $2500.00 if earnings are between $2500.00 and $5000.00, and $60.00 plus 5 percent of amount of earnings over $5000.00. Write a program segment to compute TAX given the value of earnings in EARN.

3.10 Consider the following program segment:

```
      GO TO (1,2,3,4), K
  1     K = K + 1
  2     K = K + 1
  3     K = K + 1
  4     STOP
```

If K initially is 1, 2, 3, or 4, what are its final values?
What is the final value of K if its initial value is not 1, 2,
3, or 4?

3.11  Rewrite the program segment in Figure 3.15a using
      IF statements instead of the computed GO TO.

3.12  Write a program segment that causes termination to
      occur if the value of X becomes negative and at the
      same time is less than Y.

# CHAPTER 4

# Data Input, Output, and Formatting Operations

## 4.1    INTRODUCTION

Input and output is probably the most difficult subject to master in Fortran IV. However, it is also one of the most important. The last example in Chapter 2 serves to illustrate the importance of input and output. The problem is to solve for the roots of the general quadratic equation, $Ax^2 + Bx + C = 0$.

If the solution is wanted for the roots of the particular equation $3x^2 + 5x + 2 = 0$, the program in Figure 4.1 can be used to obtain most of the desired results.

In this example, input of data for the quantities A, B, and C is supplied by the three arithmetic statements A = 3, B = 5, and C = 2. For solving this one equation, these three statements are sufficient. However, there is no provision for easily changing the values of A, B, and C in case the solution

```
A = 3
B = 5
C = 2
DIV = 2 * A
RAD = B * B − 4 * A * C
TERM1 = − B / DIV
TERM2 = SQRT (RAD) / DIV
ROOT1 = TERM1 + TERM2
ROOT2 = TERM1 − TERM2
```

**Figure 4.1 One-shot input.**

to many different equations is desired. Changing these three statements would require recompilation of the program for each set of values.

Something more flexible is needed to input values into a program other than simple arithmetic statements. Equally important is the need for the computer user to see the answers to his problem. This need is not met by the program in Figure 4.1. Therefore, the programmer must also be provided with some means of producing printed output.

## 4.2  UNFORMATTED INPUT AND OUTPUT

Some Fortran IV systems provide a simple, unformatted mode of input and output, in addition to a standard formatted mode. These simplified techniques are discussed before the more complicated mode, which is found in all Fortran IV systems.

---

4.1  Unformatted Input Statement

---

READ, *list*
where *list* represents a list of variable names.

---

Causes the computer to request input data from an input device (card reader or terminal) for listed variables.

---

he read statement, Figure
.1 modified, allowing the
, B, and C.

tement.

Fortran IV system being
will probably cause the
ossible ways:

em, the READ statement
tain the input data values
put device, such as a card

n, the READ statement
quest the data values for
at the terminal.

, the actual input data
ther in a card or at the

 = 2

resented in terms of
tinguishing them from
 following points should
tting data:

ments are not part of the
or do they become part
of the program.

2. The computer user need not know anything further
about data formats. Only the knowledge of how to

write Fortran IV constants is needed. The pseudoarithmetic statement forms a very simple link between a particular program variable name and the desired value or constant to be associated with that variable.

Now to solve the problem of producing usable printed output from a program.

---

4.2 Unformatted Output Statement

---

**PRINT**, *list*
where *list* represents a list of variable names.

---

Causes the values of the associated variables to be printed on the output device, such as a typewriter or line printer.

---

By taking the program segment of Figure 4.2 and adding an output statement, we obtain the program segment of Figure 4.3.

```
READ, A, B, C
DIV = 2 * A
RAD = B * B − 4 * A * C
TERM1 = − B / DIV
TERM2 = SQRT (RAD) / DIV
ROOT1 = TERM1 + TERM2
ROOT2 = TERM1 − TERM2
PRINT, A, B, C, ROOT1, ROOT2
```

**Figure 4.3  Output statement.**

This program segment is now capable of not only providing a flexible input technique, but also causing the computer to produce a printed copy of the answers to the original problem. The presence of the A, B, and C variables in the PRINT statement, while not necessary to obtain the roots of the equation, are useful in associating the roots with a particular set of A, B, and C values. The usefulness of this concept of "echo-checking" becomes more obvious in a few paragraphs.

The specific computer behavior caused by the PRINT statement depends on the particular Fortran IV system being used. A typical behavior is the following: Upon reaching the PRINT statement, the computer prints, either on the line printer or on the terminal typewriter, a set of pseudoarithmetic statements which define the current values associated with each of the variable names listed in the PRINT statement. Normally, the values printed out are in the same order as the variable names in the list. However, in some systems the order may vary. No problem exists, however, since each value is indentified by its variable name in the pseudoarithmetic statement. Figure 4.4 depicts the results of executing the program of Figure 4.3 under a typical conversational system. Input typed by the user is identified as such, while the rest is output from the computer.

```
BEGIN INTERPRETATION
      READ, A, B, C
a = 3, b = 5, c = 2                          ←USER INPUT
CONTINUING . . .
      PRINT, A, B, C, ROOT1, ROOT2
A = 3.0
B = 5.0
C = 2.0
ROOT1 = − 0.66666
ROOT2 = − 1.0
CONTINUING . . .
```

Figure 4.4  Program in interpretation.

```
3    READ, A, B, C
     DIV = 2 * A
     RAD = B * B - 4 * A * C
     TERM1 = - B / DIV
     TERM2 = SQRT (RAD) / DIV
     ROOT1 = TERM1 + TERM2
     ROOT2 = TERM1 - TERM2
     PRINT, A, B, C, ROOT1, ROOT2
     GO TO 3
     END
```

**Figure 4.5 Complete program example.**

To bring this program example to some kind of reasonable conclusion, a complete program is presented in Figure 4.5. Here a statement number, 3, has been placed on the first statement and an unconditional transfer statement, GO TO 3, has been added to the end of the program. To polish off the program, an END statement is added as the very last statement.

The example, in this final form, illustrates one of the techniques that makes a computer program really useful. Using a computer to solve for only one set of A, B, and C values is not very efficient. Only by using the computer's power to repeat itself rapidly, does the application become feasible.

Two minor points can be made in connection with the program in Figure 4.5

1.  This particular application does not require a STOP statement. Most computer systems are constructed so that a loop of this kind continues operating until the supply of data for the program is exhausted. Upon running out of data, the program stops as if a STOP statement had been executed.
2.  The purpose of placing A, B, and C in the PRINT statement now becomes obvious. After processing many sets of values of A, B, and C, the programmer is able to determine which values of ROOT1 and ROOT2 are associated with which values of A, B, and C.

## 4.3 FORMATTED INPUT AND OUTPUT, PRELIMINARY DISCUSSION

Input and output, in the formatted mode, is somewhat more complicated, primarily because of the necessity to specify individual formats for each input and output data item.

This involves the inclusion of one or more FORMAT statements to be used in conjunction with each input and output statement written in a program. Thus the discussion revolves around two kinds of statements. To obtain maximum clarity of the subject, both are presented in parallel. However, a series of independent definitions must be given before a meaningful discussion is initiated.

---

4.3 Unit Record

---

A unit record is usually either an
1.   80 column card or
2.   132 column line
which can be used for either input or output.

---

Each input or output operation specified by the programmer involves the transfer, either into or out of the computer, of one or more unit records. In other words, a unit record is the smallest unit of data that can be exhanged between the computer and the outside world. Even though only a portion of a card or line is needed to contain a particular set of data, the entire card or line is transferred. Another way of saying the same thing is that once the computer has looked at a card or line, it cannot look at that card or line again. Therefore, when each input or output statement is executed, new cards or lines are read or written.

---

4.4 FORMAT statement

---

FORMAT $(F_1, F_2, \ldots, F_n)$
where $F_i$ are field specifications.

---

Specifies how the unit record is to be decomposed into data fields (subdivisions) during a specific input or output operation.

---

4.5 Field Specifications

---

I*w*, E*w.d*, F*w.d*, *w*X, T*w*, *w*H ... , A*w*, and so on.

---

Specifies the type, size, and general characteristics of each particular data field that helps make up the unit record or records.

---

In general, formatted input and output is performed in the following way: The variable names involved in the input or output operation are specified by READ and WRITE statements similar to the READ and PRINT statements discussed in Section 4.2. These statements also point, by statement number, to a FORMAT statement which describes the unit record that contains, or will contain, the data being read or written. This format description allows the machine to determine what data values are associated with what variable names without resorting to the pseudoarithmetic statements used in Section 4.2.

In summary, the READ or WRITE statement specifies the variable names in the input or output operation. The FORMAT statement describes the appearance of the data which is punched or printed in the unit record.

## 4.4 FORMATTED INPUT AND OUTPUT, MAIN DISCUSSION

Formatted input and output operations are normally accomplished with the following two statements:

---

4.6 READ Statement

---

**READ (5, N)** *list*
where *N* is a FORMAT statement number and *list* is the set of variables to be read. (The 5 may change from system to system.)

---

Causes the computer to request input data from the input device (unit 5) for the listed variables. The data is read from the unit record according to the field specifications of the indicated FORMAT statement. Variables and fields are correlated one for one, from left to right.

---

4.7 WRITE Statement

---

**WRITE (6, N)** *list*
where *N* is a FORMAT statement number and *list* is the set of variables to be written. (The 6 may change from system to system.)

---

Causes the computer to write the output data on the output device (unit 6) for the listed variables. The data is written into unit records according to the field specifications of the indicated FORMAT statement. Variables and fields are correlated one for one, from left to right.

The 5 in the READ statement and the 6 in the WRITE statement are fairly standardized numbers, which indicate the computing system input and output devices, respectively.

Some Fortran IV systems allow certain variations of these statements, such as:

READ *N, list*
PRINT *N, list*

where *N* is a FORMAT statement number and the system input and output devices 5 and 6 are implied by the form of the statement.

In the following paragraphs, specific FORMAT field specifications are defined and examples of their use are given. In Section 4.5, a discussion will be presented of special and unusual conditions that occur in input and output operations.

---

4.8 Integer Field Specification

---

*alw*
where *a* is a repetition number,
I is always I,
*w* is the field width (in columns).

---

Specifies that the data appears within the field as an integer, the field being *w* columns wide and the field is repeated *a* times.

---

**Example:**

READ (5,12) I, J, K
12  FORMAT (3I10)
The unit record being read might look as follows:

| 3762 | − 335 | 72819 | _____ . . .

Column    1          11         21         31

In this example, the computer reads three values from a unit record for the three variables, I, J, and K. The unit record is composed of three fields, each ten columns wide. Thus the first field, containing a value for I, begins in column 1. The second field, containing a value for J, begins in column 11. The third field, containing a value for K, begins in column 21. The remaining columns of the unit record are unused. After the input operation is complete, I equals 3762, J equals − 335, and K equals 72819.

The data values contained within integer fields must be integers, must be read into integer variables and must be right adjusted in the field. Right adjustment means the value must be moved as far right in the field as possible, so the units digit appears in the right-most column of the field. A number which is not right adjusted is multiplied by 10 for each column out of adjustment.

An alternative way of specifying the above example is as follows:

```
      READ (5, 12) I, J, K
12    FORMAT (I 10, I 10, I 10)
```

Reading the same unit record results in obtaining the same values for I, J, and K. Thus, if the same size fields are needed, they can be so specified by using the repetition number.

To illustrate how fields of different sizes might appear, the following example is given:

```
      READ (5, 21) N, NN, M, MM
21    FORMAT (I 5, I 10, I 4, I 8)
```

The corresponding unit record might appear as:

```
         |    45|   3721|      3| 72853 |_____  . . .
Column    1      6      16     20      28
```

After the operation is completed, N equals 45, NN equals 3721, M equals 3 and MM equals 72853.

---

4.9  Real Field without Exponent Specification

---

*aFw.d*
where *a* is a repetition number,
F  is always F,
*w* is the field width in columns,
*d* is the number of decimal places in the fraction.

---

Specifies that the data appears within the field as a real number
written without an exponent, the field being *w* columns wide, the
number contains *d* fraction digits, and the field is repeated *a*
times.

---

**Example:**
         READ (5, 13) X, Y, Z
   13   FORMAT (3F10.4)

The corresponding unit record might appear as:

|       | 3.7831| 75.3000|     0.3333|     . . .
| Column    1          11          21          31

After the operation is completed, X equals 3.7831, Y
equals 75.3, and Z equals 0.3333.

Again, if field sizes are to be different, each field must
be specified separately as shown for integer fields. Unlike
integer fields, F fields do not have to contain right-adjusted
data as long as a decimal point appears within the number.
Numbers which are right-adjusted do not have to contain

decimal points. One is supplied according to the *d* parameter
in the field specification.

---

4.10  Real Field with Exponent Specification

---

*aEw.d*
where *a* is a repetition number,
**E** is always **E**,
*w* is the field width in columns,
*d* is the number of fraction digits.

---

Specifies that the data appears within the field as a real number
written with an exponent, the field being *w* columns wide, the
number contains *d* fraction digits and the field is repeated *a* times.

---

**Example:**

> READ (5,33) X, Y, Z
> 33  FORMAT (E14.5, E20.7, F10.4)

The corresponding unit record might appear as:

| 4.31846E 07 | −1.2345678E−12 | 3.1214 | . . . |
|---|---|---|---|

Column     1        15        35    45

After the operation is completed, X equals $4.31846 \times 10^7$,
Y equals $-1.2345678 \times 10^{-12}$, and Z equals 3.1214.

The E type fields must contain right-adjusted numbers,
otherwise the associated exponent is multiplied by 10 for
each column of misadjustment.

---

4.11 Column Skip Field Specification

---

*w*X

where *w* is the field width in columns.

---

Causes the computer to ignore and skip *w* columns in the unit record. This field specification does not correspond to a variable name in the READ or WRITE list.

---

**Example:**

    READ (5,6) X, Y, I
6   FORMAT (5X, F10.4, 5X, E14.6, I5)

The corresponding unit record might appear as:

```
        | 379| 786.2331| 33211| −3.753137E−03| 563|
Column    1    6         16     21                35    40          . . .
```

After the operation is completed, X equals 786.2331, Y equals − 0.003753137, and I equals 563. Columns 1 through 5 and 16 through 20 are ignored, as well as the rest of the unit record beyond 39.

Output is accomplished in much the same way as input. There is one major problem associated with output operations, but not affecting input operations; it is carriage control.

---

4.12 Carriage Control Character

---

A *blank*, a *zero*, a **1** or a **+** sign.

---

When appearing at the left-hand end of an output unit record, the carriage control characters cause the following behavior:

| | |
|---|---|
| *blank* | normal single vertical space before printing, |
| **0** | normal double vertical space before printing, |
| **1** | skip to new page before printing, |
| **+** | no space before printing. |

**Example:**
```
      WRITE (6,75) I, X
   75 FORMAT (I5, F10.4)
```

The corresponding unit record produced might appear as:

```
|     25|        0.0321|_____  . . .
```
Column  1      5               15

Two major points are made here:

1. The first field of the unit record shows up one column shorter than the specification indicated.
2. The missing character, a blank, is used as the carriage control character, thus a single vertical space is taken before the unit record is printed.

The following example illustrates these points further:

```
      WRITE (6,26) I, X
   26 FORMAT (1X, I5, F10.4)
```

The resulting unit record might appear as:

| | 25| | 0.0321| |
| --- | --- | --- | --- | --- |

`. . .`

| Column | 1 | 6 | 16 |
| --- | --- | --- | --- |

Here, the carriage control character is supplied by the 1X field, thus the I5 field is not cut short as before.

The following example is interesting for two reasons:

1. It graphically illustrates the behavior of the carriage control character.
2. It is something that should be avoided, but occurs much too often.

**Example:**

```
      I = 995
10    I = I + 1
      WRITE (6,15) I, X
15    FORMAT (I4, F10.4)
      IF (I − 2000) 10, 10, 20
```

This example produces several unit records:

| Column | 1 4 | 14 |
| --- | --- | --- |
| | 996 | 1.2345 |
| | 997 | 1.2345 |
| | 998 | 1.2345 |
| | 999 | 1.2345 |

.
.
.

REST OF PAGE

.
.
.

**NEW**

**PAGE** → ——————————————————————————————————

000       1.2345
————————————————————————————————————————

**NEW**

**PAGE** → ——————————————————————————————————

001       1.2345
————————————————————————————————————————


————————————————————————————————————————

.

.

.

The result is a stack of paper with one row of numbers on top of each page. Therefore, it should be clear that the carriage control character is obtained from the left end of the first field of an output unit record, regardless of the kind of field or its contents.

---

4.13 Literal Field Specification

---

' . . . '

where . . . represents any series of characters, except that when an apostrophe is to be included, two apostrophes are used for one.

---

Specifies a sequence of literal characters that are either:

1. Replaced by corresponding columns taken from an input unit record, or
2. Placed in the corresponding columns of an output unit record.

**Example:**

```
        WRITE (6,17) X, Y, Z
    17  FORMAT ('1X = ', F10.4,' Y = ', F8.2, ' Z = ',
        1 F8.3)
```

The resulting unit record might appear at the top of a new page as:

| X = | 35.2986 | Y = | 7261.37 | Z = | −3.456 |

Column  1    5        15    20        28    33        41

This example illustrates one way the literal field can be used to identify output data as well as to specify a particular carriage control character.

---

4.14 Hollerith Field Specification (older version of literal)

---

*w*H . . .
where *w* is the field width,
H is always H,
. . . represents any *w* characters.

---

Specifies *w* characters of literal data to be either:

1. Replaced by *w* characters from an input unit record, or
2. Placed in *w* positions of an output unit record.

---

**Example:**

```
        WRITE (6,52)
    52  FORMAT (1H1, 14X, 1HX, 14X, 1HY, 14X, 1HZ)
```

The following unit record might appear at the top of a new page as:

This technique is highly useful for producing headings above columns of data. The literal field defined previously could also be used for the same purpose. Notice here the empty list in the WRITE statement. All information being written is specified by literals.

---

4.15 Tab Field Specification

---

T*w* where *w* is the field width, and **T** is always **T**.

---

Specifies the starting column for the fields which follow, to be column *w* for input, *w* −1 for output.

---

**Example:**

```
      READ (5,34) I, X
  34  FORMAT (T30, I6, F10.4)
```

The following unit record might be read as:

```
|_____|_____4731|_____3.3197|_____ . . .
Column   1                     30      36          46
```

**Example:**

```
      WRITE (6, 29) X, Y, Z
  29  FORMAT (T32, 2F9.3, T12, F10.4)
where  X equals  8472.394,
       Y equals   392.773,
       Z equals    31.4719.
```

The following unit record is the result:

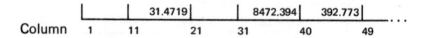

Column 1 11 21 31 40 49

Notice two points:

1. Tab fields may move the data fields from right to left.
2. On output, tab field width is one less than specified, because of the carriage control character requirement.

---

**4.16 Alphanumeric Field Specification**

---

*a*A*w*
where *a* is a repetition number,
**A** is always **A**,
*w* is the field width in columns.

---

Specifies that the data appears within the field as any combination of basic alphabetic characters, Definition 2.1, the field is to be *w* ($1 \leq w \leq 4$) columns wide, and the field is to be repeated *a* times.

---

The A field allows alphanumeric data to be read from input devices and written to output devices, while at the same time it provides the capability of referring to this type of data by variable names. Each character is stored within the machine in a special coded form, allowing 1 to 4 characters to be stored in the same space that a real or integer number requires. Thus the limitation of 4 on the field width of the A field specification is explained. Whereas ordinary arithmetic cannot be carried out with alphanumeric data, simple operations involving reading, writing, and simple replacement can be performed effectively. Return to Figure 3.15a for an example of replacement of one variable, GRADE, by one of five different alphabetic characters contained in five variable names, A, B, C, D, or E. An example of reading with an A field appears as follows:

```
      READ (5,10) A1, A2, A3, A4, A5, A6, A7, A8
  10  FORMAT (8A4)
```

These statements are used to read the following unit record:

|DATA| SET| 8, |CASE| 13,| AUG|UST |1969|
Column 1                                    33


The information read in this example could then be written by the following:

```
      WRITE (6,11) A1, A2, A3, A4, A5, A6, A7, A8
  11  FORMAT ('1', 8A4, ///)
```

The output unit record would appear at the top of a new page as:

| DATA SET 8, CASE 13, AUGUST 1969 |         . . .
Column 1                                   33



## 4.5 FORMATTED INPUT AND OUTPUT, SPECIAL CONSIDERATIONS

In order to discuss certain special problems associated with formatted input and output, the concept of format scanning must be explained. As data items are read or written to satisfy the requirements of the READ or WRITE list, corresponding format field specifications are found in the format list by a scanning process.

In order to discuss this scanning process, the following prototype of a FORMAT statement is given for reference:

```
        FORMAT((( ), ( ),...), (( ), ( ),...),...)
Level      012 2 2 2    1 12 2 2 2    1     0
```

Every FORMAT statement has one pair of level 0 parentheses opening and closing the statement. Within the level 0 parentheses, any number of sets of level 1 parentheses may appear. Within each set of level 1 parentheses, any number of sets of level 2 parentheses may appear. No higher levels are allowed. Each level 1 or 2 left parenthesis may by preceeded by a repetition number which causes the fields within the corresponding set of parentheses to be repeated.

The following points may be stated regarding the scanning process:

1. At the initiation of an input or output operation, the scan always begins with the first field following the level 0 left parenthesis.

2. The scan proceeds from left to right until the level 0 right parenthesis is encountered, in which case the scan is reflected (Figure 4.6a).

3. The level 0 right parenthesis closes out the current unit record.

4. No data transfer occurs while the scan is going from right to left.

5. The first level 1 left parenthesis encountered by a scan moving from right to left reflects the scan (Figure 4.6b).

6. A left parenthesis has no effect on a left-to-right scan, unless it is preceeded by a repetition number, in which case the fields between this left parenthesis and its mating right parenthesis are repeated the indicated number of times (Figure 4.6c).

7. A slash mark causes the current unit record to be closed out on a left-to-right scan with no reflection occurring (Figure 4.6d).

8. The slash mark has no effect on a right-to-left scan (Figure 4.6e).

9. The repetition number on a left parenthesis remains effective even if invoked by a right-to-left scan, as in point number 5.

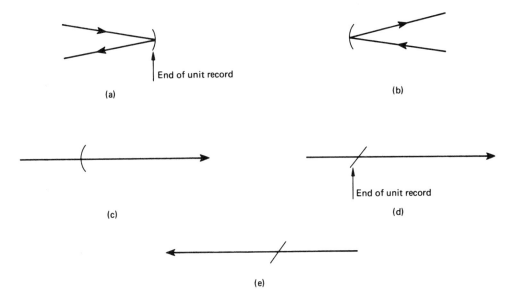

**Figure 4.6** FORMAT scanning.

The following examples illustrate some of the special effects that can be produced using these format scan characteristics.

**Example:**

        WRITE (6,7) X, Y, A, B
    7   FORMAT (F10.3, E14.5)

The two unit records produced might appear as follows:

                 5.314|   0.53894E  05|  . . .

                12.987|   0.24760E−01|  . . .
    Column   1         10              24

**Example:**

        WRITE (6,28) I, J, K, L, M
    28  FORMAT (2I10)

The three unit records produced might appear as follows:

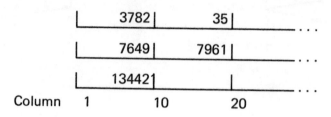

Column    1           10         20

**Example:**

       WRITE (6,35) I, J, X, K, Y
   35    FORMAT (I11/(I6,F10.4))

The three unit records produced might appear as follows:

          |       | 57387 |                 . . .

          |    27 |    37.6538 |        . . .

          |   146 |    6.7185 |         . . .

Column    1        6          16

**Example:**

       WRITE (6,14) X, A, I, B, J, Y, Z, C, K, D, L, E, F
   14    FORMAT (F11.4, 2(F8.2,I4),2F8.2)

The two unit records produced might appear as follows:
(Values are represented by their variable names)

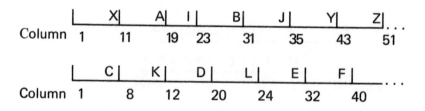

Other input and output techniques will be discussed in later chapters after further Fortran IV fundamentals have been presented.

Now, it is obvious that formatted input and output in Fortran IV is a very flexible subsystem of the language. The programmer will find that his only limitation on techniques is his own imagination.

## PRACTICE EXERCISES

4.1 Give an example of unformatted and formatted mode of input and output statements, and indicate the advantages of each.

4.2 Indicate what value is read for each set of numbers according to the corresponding format. Assume each number to be left-adjusted.

(a) 3146   F4.3            (e) 00870   F5.4
(b) 2543   I5             (f) 84003   I5
(c) 81743  F6.2            (g) 84003   F5.0
(d) 123    F3.1            (h) 84003   F5.6

4.3 Indicate a proper field specification for reading each of the following numbers from data cards.

(a) .0043                 (e) 00.00001
(b) $4.3 \times 10^{-3}$  (f) 2534100
(c) 43                    (g) 25.34
(d) 4300.00               (h) $2.5341 \times 10^6$

4.4 What is the major difference in the field specifications for input and output?

4.5 Indicate the simplest field specification for output of each of the following.

(a) 527                   (e) 2.0
(b) 824.67                (f) .02
(c) .374                  (g) $1.2 \times 10^{-3}$
(d) 3700.00               (h) $-5.3 \times 10^6$

4.6 Calculate the total number of columns used in each unit record according to the following format statements for input.

(a)   FORMAT (F5.2,10X,F3.1,I4)
(b)   FORMAT (20X,I2,10X,F5.4,E10.5)
(c)   FORMAT (1X,I1,5F4.1,E14.7)
(d)   FORMAT (10X,5I6,20X,I2)

4.7 What is the purpose of the carriage control character? Where is it located in the program and output?

4.8 Indicate what appears as output from each of the following field specifications?

(a) 'TAX='

(b) 6HCHARGE

(c) 'ANSWER 6H='

(d) 10HSTUDENT NUMBER

(e) T6, 6HANSWER, T2, 3HTHE, T13, 2HIS

(f) 'F" (X)'

(g) 4HH (X)

(h) '3HT15'

4.9 Indicate how many lines of output are produced by each of the following output statements.

(a)      WRITE(6,8) I, J, K
    8    FORMAT(3I10)
(b)      WRITE(6,8) I, J, K, X, L, M, N, Y
    8    FORMAT(I2, 2I5, F4.2)
(c)      WRITE(6,8) A, B
    8    FORMAT(F3.1,///,F4.2)
(d)      WRITE(6,3) A, B, C, D
    3    FORMAT(F3.1,///,F4.2)

4.10 Write a program to evaluate the total cost of loans ranging from $500.00 to $10,000.00 in $500.00 increments, assuming total interest rate of 6 percent. Calculate the monthly payment on the basis of a 36-month payment schedule. The output should consist of the amount borrowed, the total to be repaid, and the monthly rate. Each of the columns should have an appropriate heading.

CHAPTER **5**

# Arrays,
# the DO Statement,
# and Looping Operations

## 5.1 INTRODUCTION

A significant number of problems faced by modern computer programmers involve large quantitites of data. To make the problem even worse, each data item quite often must be distinguished uniquely from all the others. To do so by assigning a unique variable name to each data item would become very difficult. Clearly, some more reasonable way of handling this problem is needed.

Mathematically, we solve the problem to a fair degree by introducing the concepts of vector and matrix notation: In more simple terms, tables or arrays of numbers written in a formal and standardized way reduce the complexity of the problem to an acceptable level.

This chapter will be concerned with the methods used in Fortran IV to deal with large arrays of numbers. The mathematical concept of an array will be presented followed by the Fortran IV counterpart known as the subscripted variable.

Next, another control statement, the DO statement, will be presented and discussed. In conclusion, the chapter will describe the special problems to be faced in input and output of arrays.

## 5.2    VECTOR AND MATRIX NOTATION

The words vector and matrix are names applied to particular kinds of numerical arrays or tables written in a formal notation. The concept of the notation is based on the position of each number within the array. For example, consider a list of numbers represented by the following list of variable names:

$$A, B, C, D, \ldots, H.$$

The same list of names can be represented by the following list of variable names:

$$X_1, X_2, X_3, X_4, \ldots, X_m.$$

Here an integer subscript has been added to the variable name, $X$, which indicates the position of each element of the list, counting from left to right. Thus the same variable name is used to represent all the numbers in the list and yet each number is uniquely identified by its subscript.

A variable name with one associated subscript is referred to in ordinary mathematics as a vector. In general, a vector is nothing more than a one-dimensional array of numbers, or variables. Not only does the subscript notation eliminate the need for different variable names, but it also provides a means for compressing large amounts of information into smaller expressions. Thus the following statement,

$$X_1, X_2, X_3, X_4, \ldots, X_m,$$

can be written in the following way:

$$X_i, \ 1 \leq i \leq m.$$

The addition of a second subscript forms a two-dimensional array, called a matrix, which can be described as follows:

$$
\begin{array}{ccccc}
X_{1,1} & X_{1,2} & X_{1,3} & \cdots & X_{1,n} \\
X_{2,1} & X_{2,2} & X_{2,3} & \cdots & X_{2,n} \\
X_{3,1} & X_{3,2} & X_{3,3} & \cdots & X_{3,n} \\
\cdot & \cdot & \cdot & & \cdot \\
\cdot & \cdot & \cdot & & \cdot \\
\cdot & \cdot & \cdot & & \cdot \\
X_{m,1} & X_{m,2} & X_{m,3} & \cdots & X_{m,n}.
\end{array}
$$

This matrix can be further compressed to the following form:

$$X_{i,j}, \ 1 \leq i \leq m, \ 1 \leq j \leq n.$$

## 5.3 SUBSCRIPTED VARIABLES IN FORTRAN IV

Fortran IV systems usually provide means for expressing vector and matrix notations as well as tables of higher dimension. Most systems go as high as seven dimensions, thus providing the power of seven subscripts.

The only difference between the ordinary mathematical vector notation and the corresponding Fortran IV method is the inability to write below the line. Therefore, subscripts in Fortran IV are enclosed in parentheses following the variable name.

For example, the one-dimensional subscripted variable corresponding to $X_i$, is

X(I)

---

5.1 Subscripted Variable

---

Any variable name followed by one to seven expressions enclosed
by parentheses.

---

Represents a one- to seven-dimensional array of quantities, any
one of which may change during the course of computation.

---

**Examples:**

X(I,J)
MATRIX(K + 1,L,M)
TABLE(I)
ALPHA(X + Y,Z)

Subscripted variable names such as MATRIX and TABLE
shown above, can represent several kinds of numbers just as
ordinary unsubscripted variables, defined in Chapter 2. The
two kinds, as discussed before, are integer and real. The
distinction between the types is still determined by the first
letter in the name. One thing should be emphasized. All
values within an array represented by an integer name, such as
MATRIX, are of integer mode. Likewise, all values within an
array represented by a real name, such as X or TABLE, are of
real mode.

Subscripts specified for use in subscripted variables may
be any valid expression such as K + 2 or X + Y shown above.
However, when the computer goes to place values into or to
obtain values from within an array, the particular value of the
subscript is truncated to an integer. Due to this fact and
because subscripts appear more natural as integer values, most
subscript applications involve only integer mode quantities.
However, under appropriate circumstances, real expressions
can be used effectively.

Not only do most subscript expressions appear as integer
quantities, but they also appear in only a few specific forms.
The five most common forms are presented now.

For reference to a specific element in an array, the integer constant is the most logical form of subscript. Thus, in

$$X(2,3)$$

reference is being made to the one specific element at the intersection of the second row and the third column, as shown below:

Column 3
↓

$$
\begin{array}{ccccc}
X_{1,1} & X_{1,2} & X_{1,3} & \cdots & X_{1,n} \\
\text{Row 2} \rightarrow X_{2,1} & X_{2,2} & \boxed{X_{2,3}} & \cdots & X_{2,n} \\
X_{3,1} & X_{3,2} & X_{3,3} & \cdots & X_{3,n} \\
\cdot & \cdot & \cdot & & \cdot \\
\cdot & \cdot & \cdot & & \cdot \\
\cdot & \cdot & \cdot & & \cdot \\
X_{m,1} & X_{m,2} & X_{m,3} & \cdots & X_{m,n}.
\end{array}
$$

To generalize a reference to a particular dimension of an array, an integer variable is the most logical form for the subscript of the dimension being generalized. Thus in

$$X(2, J)$$

reference is being made to any of the elements in row 2, the exact element to be determined at a given time by the value of J at that time, as shown below:

$$
\begin{array}{ccccc}
X_{1,1} & X_{1,2} & X_{1,3} & \cdots & X_{1,n} \\
\text{Row 2} \rightarrow X_{2,1} & X_{2,2} & X_{2,3} & \cdots & X_{2,n} \\
X_{3,1} & X_{3,2} & X_{3,3} & \cdots & X_{3,n} \\
\cdot & \cdot & \cdot & & \cdot \\
\cdot & \cdot & \cdot & & \cdot \\
\cdot & \cdot & \cdot & & \cdot \\
X_{m,1} & X_{m,2} & X_{m,3} & \cdots & X_{m,n}
\end{array}
$$

A third common form of subscript is the skewing of a generalized reference by writing an integer variable plus or minus an integer constant. Thus, in

$$X(2,J + 3)$$

reference is being made to any of the elements in row 2, the exact element to be determined at a given time by the value of J + 3 at that time, thus skewing the reference of J by 3. The constant 3 is called a skewing constant.

A fourth common form of subscript is the skipping effect caused by writing an integer constant multiplied by an integer variable. Thus, in

$$X(2,2*J)$$

reference is being made only to the evenly numbered elements of row 2, the exact element to be determined at a given time by the value of 2*J at that time, thus skipping every other element in row 2. The constant 2 is called a skipping constant.

A fifth common form of subscript is the combination of the third and fourth forms. Thus, in

$$X(2,2*J + 3)$$

reference is being made to only the odd elements of row 2, while skewing the reference of J by 3 as well.

## 5.4 THE DIMENSION STATEMENT

Before the programmer can use subscripted variables in a program, a special specification statement must be included, the DIMENSION statement.

Any number of subscripted variables may be specified in the same DIMENSION statement. More than one DIMENSION statement may appear in the same program. The only restriction on the DIMENSION statement is that it must appear in the program prior to the use of any of the subscripted variables being specified by the statement.

---

5.2 The DIMENSION Statement

---

**DIMENSION** *V(C, C, . . . , C), V(C, C, . . . , C), . . .*
where *V* is any variable name
and *C* is an unsigned integer constant.
No more than seven *C's* can be specified for each *V*.

---

Specifies the name, dimension, and size of subscripted variables
that will be used in a program.

---

Each subscripted variable has three associated characteristics which must be defined within the DIMENSION statement:

1. The name, and thus the mode, of the variable (mode of values contained within);
2. The number of subscripts, or the dimension of each variable, limited to seven;
3. The size of each dimension, represented by the indicated maximum value of each dimension.

**Example:**

DIMENSION X(10,10), ITEM (4,5,6), A(100)

In this example, three subscripted variables are being defined:

1. X is two-dimensional with a maximum on each of its subscripts of 10. Its array contains 100 real elements, which are considered to be arranged in 10 rows and 10 columns.
2. ITEM is three-dimensional with maximums on the first, second, and third subscripts of 4, 5, and 6 respectively. Its array contains 120 integer elements, which are considered to be arranged in 6 planes of 4 rows and 5 columns each.

3.   A is one-dimensional with a maximum of 100 on its subscript. Its array contains 100 real elements.

To conclude this section, we give an example of how a subscripted variable can be used. Here a table of values is assumed to exist in the one-dimensional subscripted variable, X. The object is to determine the value, represented by BIG, of the largest element in the table. It is further assumed that the table contains 100 values.

```
      DIMENSION X(100)
           .
           .
           .
      BIG = X(1)
      I = 2
 1    IF(X(I) − BIG) 3,3,2
 2    BIG = X(I)
 3    I = I + 1
      IF(I − 100) 1, 1, 4
 4         .
           .
           .
```

An analysis of this example may prove helpful to some readers.

The statement, BIG = X(1), is an assumption that the first element in X is the largest, thus providing a starting point in the search portion of the program beginning with the statement numbered 1.

Due to the above assumption, the search for the largest element begins with a subscript value of 2, thus the statement I = 2.

The four statements, beginning with the statement numbered 1, comprise a loop which searches through the table, X, for the largest element. The statement numbered 1, " IF(X(I) − BIG) 3,3,2" compares the largest element found so far during the search with the element currently being pointed to by I. If the current element X(I) is larger than BIG, the largest element found so far, control passes to the statement whose number is 2. Here the value of BIG is replaced by X(I) which becomes the new largest element found so far. If the current element X(I) is smaller than or equal to BIG, control is passed to the statement whose number is 3, bypassing the statement that changes BIG.

Regardless of whether or not the statement numbered 2 is executed, control reaches statement 3, where the current value of I is increased by 1. The next statement, "IF(I − 100) 1,1,4" determines the end of the search. As long as I remains less than or equal to 100, control returns to the statement numbered 1. Upon I reaching a value of 101, control passes to the statement numbered 4 and leaves the loop behind. When the loop is completed, the variable BIG is equal to the largest element of X(I).

## 5.5 THE DO STATEMENT

One classical technique in programming which can be analyzed and discussed in a classical sense is the loop. All loops seem to have four distinct parts or sections: (1) initializing, (2) processing, (3) incrementing, and (4) testing. The loop in the example shown in Section 5.4 is typical and can be described as follows:

| | |
|---|---|
| Initializing ← | BIG = X(1) |
| | I = 2 |
| Processing ← | 1 IF(X(I) − BIG) 3,3,2 |
| | 2 BIG = X(I) |
| Incrementing ← | 3 I = I + 1 |
| Testing ← | IF (I − 100) 1,1,4 |

The initializing section normally appears first and is used to initialize all necessary variables to their proper values for use in the loop which follows.

The processing section appears second and is the portion of the loop which accomplishes the task or tasks for which the loop is designed.

The incrementing section appears third. In this simple example, I is incremented by one to count the number of iterations that have been performed.

The fourth and final section, the testing section, checks to see when the loop is completed. Until it is completed, control is returned to the beginning of the loop, or the statement numbered 1. When the number of iterations reaches the upper limit, in this case 101, control passes to the statement numbered 4, completing the loop.

Fortran IV provides a statement which combines three of the four sections of a loop into one statement, the DO statement.

---

5.3  The DO Statement

---

**DO** $N$ $I = M_1, M_2, M_3$
where $N$ is a statement number appearing physically below the **DO** statement.
$I$ is an integer variable. $M_i$ are either unsigned integer variables or unsigned integer constants.
$M_3$ is optional and is assumed to be 1 if it is omitted.

---

Indicates that the statements below the **DO** down through the statement whose number is $N$, called the range, are to be repeated; the first time with $I$, called the index, equal to $M_1$, the initial value; each successive time $I$ is to be increased by $M_3$, called the increment; and to be continued until $I$ is about to exceed $M_2$, the upper limit.

---

Thus, the DO statement combines the initializing, incrementing, and testing sections into one statement. A counting variable, called the Index of the DO, is automatically initialized, incremented and tested for completion. The following diagram provides a general picture of the DO statement.

The value of I changes on each repetition or iteration of the statements in the range, as shown in the following table:

| Interation | Value of I |
|---|---|
| 1 | $M_1$ |
| 2 | $M_1 + M_3$ |
| 3 | $M_1 + 2M_3$ |
| . | . |
| . | . |
| . | . |
| LAST | $M_2 - M_3 < I \leq M_2$ |

The LAST iteration count is computed from $((M_2 - M_1)/M_3) + 1$, where the ratio is truncated to an integer.

As further illustration of the DO, the following two program segments are equivalent:

DO $N$ I = $M_1$, $M_2$, $M_3$          I = $M_1$

‾‾‾‾‾‾‾‾‾‾‾‾‾    1 ‾‾‾‾‾‾‾‾‾‾‾‾‾

‾‾‾‾‾‾‾‾‾‾‾‾‾ = ‾‾‾‾‾‾‾‾‾‾‾‾‾

N ‾‾‾‾‾‾‾‾‾‾‾‾‾    N ‾‾‾‾‾‾‾‾‾‾‾‾‾

I = I + $M_3$
IF(I − $M_2$) 1,1,2

2

As a specific example, the program of Section 5.4 is now shown using a DO statement:

```
        DIMENSION X(100)
                 .
                 .
                 .
        BIG = X(1)
        DO 2 I = 2, 100
        IF(X(I) − BIG) 2,2,1
    1   BIG = X(I)
    2   CONTINUE
                 .
                 .
                 .
```

This example also illustrates a use for the dummy statement, CONTINUE. This statement is useful when a statement number is needed to which control can be passed but in which no operation is to be performed. The problem arises at the time when one of the alternative paths inside a DO loop needs to transfer to the incrementing and testing sections of the classical loop.

## 5.6 GENERAL COMMENTS ABOUT DO STATEMENTS

It should be emphasized that all parameters or quantities used in a DO statement must be expressed as integer quantities. Also the upper limit normally should be greater than the initial value. No signs may be used for any quantity and usually an initial value of zero is not allowed.

A DO is said to be *satisfied* when the index becomes equal to the upper limit or is about to exceed the upper limit. Upon satisfaction, control leaves ("falls through") the DO range and continues with the statement following the last statement in the range.

The index quantity is always available for use as a subscript, for general computation or as a counter without any explicit reference to the index, outside the DO statement itself, during the execution of the statements within the range of the DO. However, the value of the index after satisfaction is usually unpredictable.

The range of one DO may contain other DO's, a process called nesting. Within a nest, however, the range of the innermost DO must be completely within the range of the overlapping DO or DO's. Any number of DO's, within reason, may be nested. The index of the innermost DO varies the most often, while the index of the outermost DO varies the least often. Several DO ranges may terminate on the same statement.

Transfers may be made out of a DO range but should not be made into a DO range from outside the range. In other words, entry into a DO range should always be by way of the DO statement itself.

A DO range may not terminate on another DO, any transfer statement, or any specification statement. The CONTINUE statement may be used to terminate a DO in those instances where a transfer statement might appear to be the end of the DO range.

The number of iterations specified by a DO statement with the general parameters, $M_1$, $M_2$, and $M_3$, may be computed using the following formula:

$$N = ((M_2 - M_1)/M_3) + 1$$

where the ratio is performed in integer arithmetic, so that the quotient is truncated to the next lowest integer (called the floor function). (Incidentally, rounding up to an integer is called the ceiling function.)

## 5.7 INPUT AND OUTPUT CONSIDERATIONS FOR ARRAYS

Fortran IV contains a feature which is highly useful in the input and output of arrays. The feature is called the implied DO and may be used in input and output statements as in the following example:

```
      READ(5,7) (X(I), I = 1,100)
7     FORMAT(10F8.2)
```

These two statements cause 100 values to be read from 10 data cards, 10 values each, into the subscripted variable, X(I).

A very important point is illustrated by the following example:

```
        DO 6 I = 1,100
   6    READ(5,7) X(I)
   7    FORMAT(10F8.2)
```

Unlike the previous example, these three statements cause the 100 values to be read from 100 data cards, 1 value each. The reason is that the READ statement is being executed, from scratch, 100 separate times, thus initiating a new unit record each time. In the previous example, the READ statement is executed only once, thus the 10 data cards are under the control of the FORMAT statement.

Several levels of implied DO's may be specified in the same statement, as in the following example:

```
        READ(5,7) ((X(I,J),I = 1,10),J = 1,10)
   7    FORMAT(10F8.2)
```

In this example, 100 values are read from 10 data cards for the subscripted variable, X(I,J). Notice that the I subscript varies most often; its implied DO is the innermost. The implied DO's cause the data values to be read into the matrix (two-dimensional subscripted variable) in column-wise order, as described by the following sequence:

$$X_{1,1}, X_{2,1}, X_{3,1}, \ldots, X_{1,2}, X_{2,2}, X_{3,2}, \ldots, X_{1,n}, X_{2,n}, X_{3,n}, \ldots, X_{m,n}.$$

This sequence is called *natural order*, even though a row-wise sequence might seem more natural. If natural order is the order desired, Fortran IV provides another feature, illustrated in the following example:

```
        DIMENSION X(10,10)
                    .
                    .
                    .
        READ (5,7) X
   7    FORMAT(10F8.2)
```

In this example, Fortran IV recognizes the X to be subscripted and performs the same operation as was indicated in the previous example. Thus when the natural-order implied DO sequencing is desired, only the name of the variable need be written. One note of caution, the system uses the maximum subscript values given in the DIMENSION statement as the upper limit values in the implied DO's.

The same remarks apply to output as well as input, except, of course, that the carriage control character must be accounted for.

One final example is given to illustrate how to obtain a printout of a matrix in matrix form. Implied DO's must be used to specify the order, since natural order inverts the natural appearance of a matrix:

```
        WRITE(6,7) ((X(I,J),J = 1,10),I = 1,10)
7       FORMAT(10F10.4)
```

In this particular example, the following is equivalent:

```
        DO 6 I = 1,10
6       WRITE(6,7) (X(I,J),J = 1,10)
7       FORMAT(10F10.4)
```

However, the following is not equivalent for the same reason as in a previous example:

```
        DO 6 I = 1,10
        DO 6 J = 1,10
6       WRITE(6,7) X(I,J)
7       FORMAT(10F10.4)
```

## 5.8 COMPREHENSIVE EXAMPLE

The following simple payroll problem is presented as a comprehensive example of how subscripted variables can be used effectively.

```
        DIMENSION  HOURS(7,100),  TLTHRS(100),
      1 RATE(100), PAY(100)
        DO 1 I = 1, 100
        TLTHRS(I) = 0.0
        RATE(I) = 0.0
        PAY(I) = 0.0
        DO 1 J = 1, 7
1       HOURS(J, I) = 0.0
2       READ (5,3) ID, X
3       FORMAT(I3, F5.2)
        IF(ID) 5, 5, 4
4       RATE(ID) = X
        GO TO 2
5       READ (5,6) ID, IDAY, HRS
6       FORMAT(I3, I1, F5.2)
        IF(ID) 8, 8, 7
7       HOURS(IDAY, ID) = HRS
        GO TO 5
8       DO 13 I = 1, 100
        CUTOFF = 8.0
        DO 12 J = 1, 7
        OVRTIM = 0.0
        IF(J − 5) 10, 10, 9
9       CUTOFF = 0.0
10      DIFF = HOURS (J, I) - CUTOFF
        IF(DIFF) 12, 12, 11
11      OVRTIM = DIFF / 2.0
12      TLTHRS(I)  =  TLTHRS(I)  +  HOURS(J,I)  +
      1 OVRTIM
13      PAY(I) = TLTHRS(I) * RATE(I)
        WRITE (6,14)
14      FORMAT('1 EMPLOYEE ID ', 5X, ' HOURS ', 5X,
      1 ' PAY ' //)
        TOTAL = 0.0
        DO 17 I = 1, 100
        IF(PAY(I)) 17, 17, 15
15      TOTAL = TOTAL + PAY(I)
        WRITE (6,16) I, TLTHRS(I), PAY(I)
16      FORMAT(I10, F20.1, F10.2)
17      CONTINUE
        WRITE (6,18) TOTAL
```

```
18  FORMAT ('1 TOTAL SALARIES PAID ', F10.2)
    STOP
    END
```

The program is designed to be run on a weekly basis. Provisions are made to accomodate seven working days and to allow for possible overtime. Overtime hours are computed as 1.5 times the amount over 8 hours on week days and 1.5 times any hours on the weekends.

The program contains four subscripted variables, as seen in the DIMENSION statement. HOURS contains the actual hours worked on a daily basis. The table is set up for a maximum of 100 employees. The first dimension represents the seven days of the week. TLTHRS contains the total hours worked by each employee after adjustment for overtime. RATE contains the pay scale, measured in dollars per hour. PAY equals the total salary for each employee. Each employee has an ID number between 1 and 100 which is used for subscript control in the arrays.

The logical flow of the program is as follows:

1. The first six executable statements clear out all data tables.
2. The next five statements read in the data for each employee's pay rate. The end of this data file is indicated by a zero ID number (a blank card is a handy device for providing a zero field).
3. The next five statements read in the data for daily hours worked by each employee. Again, a zero ID indicates the end of the file.
4. Statements numbered 8 through 13 are the ones responsible for computing total hours worked and the pay for each employee. Notice how some statements are inside two DO loops, while some are inside only one. Those computations depending on the day of the week are inside both DO loops. Those computations which are independent of the day (for the entire week) are inside only one DO.
5. The balance of the program is used to print out a table of employee ID numbers, hours worked, and weekly salary. Finally, the total of all salaries is printed.

Thus, from this brief set of examples, the reader should be able to envision more sophisticated applications of arrays and how to perform input and output operations involving arrays. Again, the programmer is limited only by his own imagination.

One final remark might be made with respect to subscripted variables and their use. Basically, before a programmer resorts to using a subscripted variable, there should be a compelling reason why all the quantities to be placed in an array must be within the machine at the same time. If such a reason does not exist, the use of subscripted variables only complicates the problem.

## PRACTICE EXERCISES

5.1 Write detailed arrays indicating how each of the following subscripted variables is organized.

(a) A(I), $1 \leq I \leq 10$;

(b) B(I, J), $1 \leq I \leq 5$, $1 \leq J \leq 6$;

(c) C(I, J), $1 \leq I \leq 3$, $1 \leq J \leq 10$;

(d) D(I, J), $1 \leq I \leq 4$, $1 \leq J \leq 4$;

(e) E(I, J, K), $1 \leq I \leq 2$, $1 \leq J \leq 2$, $1 \leq K \leq 2$.

5.2 Given a two-dimensional array called X of 10 rows and 10 columns. Indicate correct subscript expressions for each of the following (use I for row and J for column subscript values):

(a) Any element in column 4,

(b) Any element in row 6,

(c) Any element of entire matrix,

(d) Specifically the intersection of row 3 and column 7,

(e) Any element of row 5 skewed by 3,

(f) Every third element of column 6,

(g) Any element in odd rows and even columns,

(h) Even elments of row 3 skewed by 2.

5.3 Write a DIMENSION statement defining the subscripted variables described in Problems 5.1 and 5.2.

5.4 Determine the number of elements in each of the subscripted variables described in Problems 5.1 and 5.2.

5.5 Rewrite the program in Section 5.4 assuming X is a 10 by 10 matrix. The object is to find the largest element in the entire array.

5.6 Rewrite the program in Section 5.4 to find the smallest element in the array.

5.7 In each of the following DO statements, determine all parameters and compute the number of iterations each would cause:

(a) DO 3 I = 1,10          (d) DO 5 L = 5,100,5
(b) DO 7 J = 2,15,2        (e) DO 8 M = 10,100,3
(c) DO 16 K = 1,50,3       (f) DO 6 N = 1,1000,9

5.8 Show how each of the DO statements in Problem 5.7 could be replaced with an IF statement and two arithmetic statements.

5.9 Rewrite the program of Problem 5.5 using DO statements.

5.10 Write input and FORMAT statements to read in values for the subscripted variables in Problem 5.1. Use DO statements for one method, and implied DO's for another method.

5.11 A two-dimensional subscripted variable called ARRAY contains 5 rows and 7 columns. Write a program segment which will print the heading MATRIX ARRAY, followed by two blank lines, and then list the values of the array in normal matrix fashion with 5 lines of 7 values each.

5.12 What does the following program do? What does *natural order* mean? How does the printed output compare with the input?

```
      DIMENSION A(5, 5)
      READ(5,1) ((A(I,J),J=1,5),I=1,5)
1     FORMAT(5F8.4)
      DO 2 L=1,5
      DO 2 M=1,5
      ASAVE=A(L,M)
      A(L,M)=A(M,L)
2     A(M,L)=ASAVE
      WRITE(6,3) A
3     FORMAT(' ',5F8.4)
      STOP
      END
```

CHAPTER **6**

# Functions, Subroutines, and Associated Operations

## 6.1 INTRODUCTION

Fortran IV systems provide means to segment a large program into several smaller subprograms, thus reducing the complexity of solving certain problems. A reason, other than simplification, for segmenting a program is the high probability of finding a program already written, which solves the portion of the problem in question. Examples of such programs are the supplied functions like SQRT and SIN. The efficient numerical techniques for evaluating these functions are somewhat difficult and not well known. However, because of their occurrence in many problems, they are provided as standard program segments in most Fortran IV systems. A third reason, and perhaps the most valid one, for segmenting a program into subprograms is the ability to use or call a particular subprogram segment any number of times from different places within the main program or procedure. This availability not only provides economy in time and effort in writing a program, but also allows fewer chances of error. This chapter will present the methods provided in Fortran IV for defining and using the programmer's own functions or subroutines, the two kinds of subprograms.

A general diagram (Figure 6.1) may more clearly illustrate the points just made.

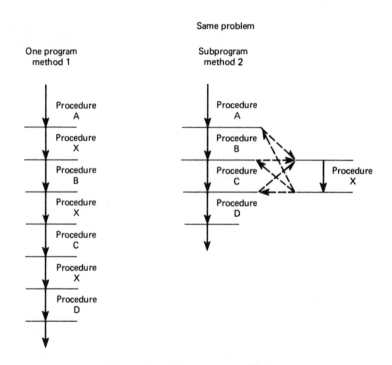

Figure 6.1 Subprogram technique.

## 6.2 FORTRAN IV SUBPROGRAMS

Definitions 6.1 and 6.2 provide a precise description of subprograms and main programs.

---

6.1 Subprogram

---

A set of Fortran IV statements beginning with either of the two statements
**FUNCTION** or **SUBROUTINE**
and ending with the **END** statement.

---

Logically, a group of statements which solve only a portion of a problem; used or *called* by a main program or other subprograms.

---

6.2 Main Program

---

A set of Fortran IV statements *not* beginning with either of the two statements
**FUNCTION** or **SUBROUTINE**
and ending with the **END** statement.

---

Logically, a group of statements which either completely solves a problem by itself or solves only a portion of a problem, in which case it may *call* or use a subprogram to complete the solution wholly or partially.

---

Thus, a main program can be an independent procedure for solving a particular problem, or it may depend on subprograms for partially solving the problem, although subprograms are not mandatory.

A subprogram, on the other hand, is totally dependent on either a main program or other subprograms to call it into use. Definitions 6.3 and 6.4 establish the relationship between *calling* and *called* programs.

---

6.3 A *calling* Program

Either a main program or subprogram which *calls* a subprogram using a standardized *calling* procedure.

---

6.4 A *called* Program

A subprogram which is being *called* by either a main program or a subprogram using a standardized *calling* procedure.

---

Figure 6.2 illustrates the principle of subprogram calling in Fortran IV. The same principle can be applied to any number of subprograms as well as the main program. Figure 6.3 illustrates a variation of the same theme.

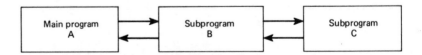

Program A calls subprogram B
Subprogram B calls subprogram C
Subprogram B is called by program A
Subprogram C is called by subprogram B

**Figure 6.2  Calling sequence.**

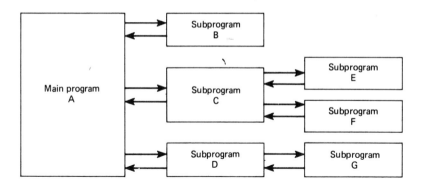

A calls B, C or D
C calls E or F
D calls G
B, C, or D is called by A
E or F is called by C
G is called by D

**Figure 6.3  Calling sequences.**

One note of caution, Fortran IV does not allow recursion in subprogram calling, that is, a subprogram may not call itself, either directly or indirectly. Thus, a sequence of subprogram calls must not form a loop, regardless of how many subprograms are involved. Also, all returns of subprogram calls must be along the path of the original call. Thus, in Figure 6.3, subprogram E must return control to subprogram C before returning control to the main program, A.

Function and subroutine subprograms differ slightly in definition, but significantly in use. Thus, each type is presented separately even though there is some overlap in discussion.

There are two major considerations in the design and use of every subprogram:

1. The definition of the procedure used in the function or subroutine,
2. How the subprogram is referenced in the calling program.

## 6.3 FUNCTION SUBPROGRAMS

Definition 6.5 describes the requirements for writing a function subprogram in Fortran IV. Definition 6.6 describes how a function subprogram is called from the calling program.

---

6.5 FUNCTION Subprogram

---

Represented by a set of Fortran IV statements beginning with the statement
**FUNCTION** *NAME (ARG1, ARG2, . . . )*
and ending with **END** and usually containing one or more **RETURN** statements. *NAME* is a symbol and *ARG*1, *ARG*2, . . . are variable names.

---

Defines a procedure for evaluating a particular function involving the arguments specified in the **FUNCTION** statement and having only one value as a result.

---

6.6 Calling a FUNCTION Subprogram

---

Indicated by placing within any arithmetic expression the name of the function and followed by one or more arguments enclosed in parentheses. The name is specified by the FUNCTION statement appearing at the beginning of the corresponding subprogram.

---

Connects calling and called programs, transferring control to and from the called subprogram, transferring arguments to the subprogram, and transferring the result back to the calling program.

---

---

6.7 RETURN Statement

---

**RETURN**

---

Indicates that control is to be returned from the called subprogram back to the calling program, normally at the point of the original call.

---

The name of the function subprogram is arbitrary and is created by the programmer. The mode of the result is indicated by the *NAME*, just as in ordinary variable names, thus some care must be exercised by the user. To illustrate the definition and use of a function subprogram, the following example is used. Suppose the following relationships are required in a program:

$$F\ (X)\ =\ \begin{cases} X-1, & 1 \le X \\ 1-X^2, & X \le 1. \end{cases}$$

The program segments in Figure 6.4 define and use the function subprogram technique to implement the above relationship.

Referring to the function subprogram definition in Figure 6.4, we can make the following observations: Upon entry into the subprogram, the value of the argument X is transferred from the calling program into the subprogram for use during the execution of the subprogram. Execution normally begins with the first statement after the function statement and continues in natural sequence. In this particular example, if the value of $X$ is less than 1.0, $F$ is set equal to $1.0 - X^2$ and control is then returned to the calling program. If $X$ is greater than or equal to 1.0, then $F$ is set equal to $X - 1.0$ and control is returned to the calling program. In either case, the resulting value of $F$ is carried back to the calling program and substituted into the expression from which the original call was made.

| Subprogram Definition | Main Program Use |
|---|---|
| | A = · · · |
| | SUM = · · · |
| | Y = · · · |
| | Z = · · · |
| | . |
| | . |
| | . |
| FUNCTION F(X) | 1  RESULT = A * F(Y+Z) |
| IF(X−1.0) 1, 2, 2 | . |
| 1 F = 1.0 − X ** 2 | ANGLE = · · · |
| RETURN | . |
| 2 F = X − 1.0 | 2  ALPHA = F(ANGLE) / 3.0 |
| RETURN | . |
| END | DX = · · · |
| | . |
| | 3  SUM = SUM + F(DX) |
| | . |
| | . |
| | . |
| | END |

**Figure 6.4** FUNCTION subprogram.

Referring to the main program in Figure 6.4, the behavior can be described as follows: During the evaluation of the expression in the statement numbered 1, a call to the subprogram F is made. The value of Y+Z is transferred into the subprogram as the value of X. Upon returning from the subprogram with the appropriate value of F, evaluation of the same expression continues by multiplying the value of F by the value of A, yielding the value for the variable RESULT. Upon reaching the statement numbered 2, a second call to the subprogram F is made. This time the argument X is made equal to the value of ANGLE. The value of the function F upon return is divided by 3 and stored as the value of ALPHA. A third call is made in statement numbered 3, where the argument is the value of DX, and the functional value F is used to increase the current value of SUM.

The following general characteristics of function sub-programs should be emphasized:

1. One or more arguments must be specified for a function.
2. The mode of the arguments in the calling program must correspond to those in the called program.
3. Only one answer can be computed by a function subprogram.
4. If the same variable names appear in both calling and called programs they are entirely independent except for the names that appear in the argument lists, in which case they are essentially made equivalent.

The example in Figure 6.5 illustrates point 4.

| Subprogram | Main Program |
|---|---|
| FUNCTION FUN(A) | Y = · · · |
| A = 2 * A | · |
| B = 2 * A | · |
| FUN = 2 * A**3 + 5 | X = FUN(Y) |
| RETURN | DATA = B * X |
| END | · |
| | · |
| | · |
| | END |

**Figure 6.5** FUNCTION **containing a possible error.**

The subprogram in Figure 6.5 might be considered to have a rather strange effect on the variable Y in the main program. Because Y in the main program is essentially equivalent to A in the subprogram, the presence of A on the left-hand side of the equal sign in the subprogram changes the value of Y in the main program. Therefore the arguments of a function call should not normally appear on the left of an equal sign in the function subprogram itself. However, variables, such as B, not in the argument list but still in both subprogram and main program are independent. Changing B in the subprogram thus has no effect on the value of B in the main program. The system protects the two B values as though the variable names were actually different.

## 6.4 SUBROUTINE SUBPROGRAMS

Even though function subprograms provide a very flexible extension of the Fortran IV language, there is still a limitation which is eliminated with the introduction of the subroutine subprogram. There can be any number of results, or none at all, computed and returned by the subroutine subprogram. This new flexibility forces the subroutine subprogram to become involved in the language in a way different from that of the functions, particularly in the way in which calls are made to subroutines. Obviously, no more than one value can be substituted into an expression at a given point. Therefore, a new statement, the CALL statement, is introduced to answer this problem.

---

6.8 SUBROUTINE Subprogram

---

A set of Fortran IV statements beginning with
**SUBROUTINE** *NAME (ARG1, ARG2, . . . )*
ending with the **END** statement, and usually containing one or more **RETURN** statements. *NAME* is a symbol and *ARG1*, *ARG2*, . . . are variable names.

---

Specifies a procedure for solving a portion of a particular problem.

---

6.9 The CALL Statement

---

**CALL** *NAME (ARG*1, *ARG*2, ... )
where *NAME* is the name of a corresponding subroutine subprogram and *ARG*1, *ARG*2, ... are arguments which correspond to the arguments used in the subroutine subprogram definition.

---

Specifies that control be transferred to the subroutine subprogram along with appropriate arguments. At the completion of the subroutine action, control is normally returned to the calling program at the statement following the **CALL** statement with any appropriate output or result arguments.

---

The arguments passed during a subroutine subprogram CALL or RETURN can be either input arguments to be used during the execution of the subprogram, or output arguments to represent any results computed by the subroutine subprogram. Thus the result is not returned by the name of the subroutine, as in the case of function subprograms.

The example shown in Figure 6.6 involves a subroutine subprogram designed to find the largest element in a given row of a matrix and to return the value and column number.

Here, statement 10 calls subroutine BIG to find the largest element, XMAX, of column K in the third row of matrix DATA. Statement 20 calls the same subroutine to find the largest element, XYZ, of column ICOL in the seventh row of matrix DATA. Statement 100, within a DO loop, causes the subroutine to be called 10 times to find the largest element in each row of matrix DATA. The values of the largest elements are stored in X(I) and the corresponding column numbers are stored in MAX(I).

Again, as in function subprograms, variables appearing as arguments are made equivalent between the calling program

| Subroutine | Main Program |
|---|---|
| SUBROUTINE BIG(X,I,A,N) | DIMENSION DATA(10,10) |
| DIMENSION X(10,10) | DIMENSION MAX(10), X(10) |
| A = X(I,1) | . |
| | . |
| N = 1 | . |
| DO 2 J = 2, 10 | 10 CALL BIG(DATA,3,XMAX,K) |
| IF(A−X(I,J)) 1, 2, 2 | . |
| | . |
| 1 N = J | . |
| A = X(I,J) | 20 CALL BIG(DATA,7,XYZ,ICOL) |
| 2 CONTINUE | . |
| | . |
| RETURN | . |
| END | DO 100 I = 1, 10 |
| | 100 CALL BIG(DATA,I,X(I),MAX(I)) |
| | . |
| | . |
| | . |
| | END |

Figure 6.6 SUBROUTINE subprogram.

and the subroutine subprogram. Variables having the same names in the calling program and subroutine subprogram, but not appearing in the argument list, are independent as if they had unique names.

Dimensions specified by DIMENSION statements within subprograms may be indicated by variable names. However, a specific value must be provided at execution time by argument transmission from the calling program. Thus, the DIMENSION in the subroutine in Figure 6.6 could appear as

DIMENSION X(M,N)

provided that arguments are included in the calling sequence which make M and N equal to specific values during execution. Therefore, the dimensions adjust to the demands dynamically.

## 6.5 MULTIPLE ENTRIES IN SUBPROGRAMS

More than one entry into a function or subroutine subprogram is specified by an ENTRY statement.

---

6.10 ENTRY Statement

---

**ENTRY** *NAME (ARG1, ARG2, ... )*
where *NAME* is the name of the entry point and *ARG1*, *ARG2*,... are arguments to be transferred to or from the subprogram. *NAME* is a symbol and *ARG1, ARG2,...* are variable names.

---

Specifies a separate and unique entry point into the subprogram.

---

An example of the use of ENTRY is shown in Figure 6.7.

| Subroutine | Main Program |
|---|---|
| SUBROUTINE X(A,B) | . |
| . | . |
| . | CALL X(P,Q) |
| ENTRY Y(A,B,C) | . |
| . | . |
| . | CALL Z(Q,R) |
| ENTRY Z(A,B) | . |
| . | . |
| . | CALL Y(P,Q,R) |
| END | . |
| | . |
| | END |

**Figure 6.7 Multiple entries.**

The effect of multiple entries is like having several subprograms combined into a single subprogram. In other words, an ENTRY statement is treated in the same way as FUNCTION or SUBROUTINE statements with respect to the calling procedure. In addition, computations made in a subprogram on one entry could depend upon computations made during prior entries, either at the same entry or at different entries.

## 6.6  VARIABLE RETURNS IN SUBROUTINE SUBPROGRAMS

Returns from subroutine subprograms may specify a variable return point. A variation of the RETURN statement is used. Figure 6.8 is an illustration of this technique.

---

6.11  Variable RETURN Statement

---

**RETURN** *I*

where *I* is an unsigned integer constant or variable.

---

Specifies that the return is to be made to the *i*th statement number given in the argument list of the respective CALL statement.

---

The behavior in Figure 6.8 is as follows: Three statement numbers are written within the argument list of the CALL statement, each one preceded by an ampersand (&) to distinguish the element as being a statement number rather than a simple constant. Asterisks appear within the argument list of the corresponding subroutine statement in the positions used by the ampersand statement numbers in the CALL statement. With this preparation, the combination of the GO TO and the RETURN *I* statements in the subroutine causes

| Subroutine | Main Program |
|---|---|
| SUBROUTINE A(X,Y,*,*,*) | . |
| . | . |
| . | CALL A(P,Q,&4,&8,&3) |
| K = · · · | Y = Q + Y |
| GO TO(10,20,30,40),K | . |
| 10  RETURN | . |
| 20  RETURN 1 | 4 Y = Q + 2*Y |
| 30  RETURN 2 | . |
| 40  RETURN 3 | 3 Y = Q + 3*Y |
| END | . |
| | . |
| | . |
| | 8 Y = Q + 6*Y |
| | . |
| | . |
| | END |

**Figure 6.8  Variable returns.**

the actual return to the calling program at different points within the calling program. In the above example, if K in the subroutine is equal to 1, return is made to the statement following the CALL. If K is equal to 2, return is made to statement 4 in the calling program. If K is equal to 3, statement 8 is the return point, just as statement 3 is the return point for a value of K equal to 4.

## 6.7  THE EXTERNAL STATEMENT

In certain problems a programmer may wish to pass a subprogram name to a function or subroutine, rather than a value, as has been presented in all of the above discussions. In order to pass names as arguments, the names must be defined as being such by the use of an EXTERNAL statement.

| |
|---|
| 6.12 The EXTERNAL Statement |
| **EXTERNAL** *A, B, C, . . .*<br>where *A, B, C, . . .* are the names of subprograms. |
| Specifies that the listed names are to be passed as arguments to other subprograms. |

Figure 6.9 illustrates how the EXTERNAL statement is used to provide an additional measure of flexibility to Fortran IV.

| Subroutine | Main Program |
|---|---|
| | . |
| | . |
| | EXTERNAL SIN, COS |
| SUBROUTINE SUB(A,B,C,X) | . |
| A = X(B+C) | . |
| RETURN | CALL SUB (X,Y,Z,SIN) |
| END | . |
| | . |
| | CALL SUB (X,Y,Z,COS) |
| | . |
| | . |
| | END |

**Figure 6.9** EXTERNAL references.

The effect here is to cause the subroutine to evaluate the following relationship on the first call:

$$X = SIN(Y+Z)$$

while on the second call, the following relationship is evaluated:

$$X = COS(Y+Z)$$

where X, Y, and Z are the variables used in the main program.

## 6.8 THE COMMON STATEMENT

Another specification statement, which is useful in subprogram programming, is the COMMON statement. Through its use, arguments are eliminated from the CALL, FUNCTION, and SUBROUTINE statements.

---

6.13  The COMMON Statement

---

COMMON */NAME1/ A1, B1, . . . /NAME2/ A2, B2, . . .*
where *NAME1, NAME2, . . .* are optional **COMMON** block names and *A1, B1, . . . , A2, B2, . . .* are variable names (subscripted or not).

---

Specifies that *A1, B1, . . .* are to be located in a **COMMON** area of storage called *NAME1, A1, B2, . . .* are to be located in a **COMMON** area called *NAME2*, and so forth. If *NAME* is omitted, then the corresponding variables are placed in an unlabeled area of **COMMON** storage.

---

When COMMON statements are placed in calling and called programs, variables in the calling and called programs are placed into COMMON storage areas. This eliminates the need to pass arguments to and from subprograms.

In addition, DIMENSION statement information may be incorporated into the COMMON statement.

Figure 6.10 illustrates a use for the COMMON statement.

| Subroutines | Main Program |
|---|---|
| SUBROUTINE SUB1(. . .) | · |
| COMMON E,F/X/G,H | · |
| · | COMMON A,B/X/U,V/Y/W |
| · | · |
| END | · |
| | · |
| SUBROUTINE SUB2(. . .) | CALL SUB1(. . .) |
| COMMON P,Q /Y/R | · |
| · | CALL SUB2(. . .) |
| · | · |
| END | · |
| | END |

**Figure 6.10** COMMON statements.

In‑ this example, the variables A and B in the main program are made equivalent to E and F in subroutine SUB1 and P and Q in subroutine SUB2 through the use of only two locations in unlabeled COMMON storage. In a COMMON area called X, the variables U and V in the main program are stored in COMMON locations with G and H in subroutine SUB1. In a COMMON area called Y, the variable W in the main program is stored in a COMMON location with the variable R in subroutine SUB2. Therefore, none of these variables need to appear in argument lists within the calling sequences.

Several COMMON statements may appear in the same program; the effect is a cumulative one. Thus, the two statements

COMMON X, Y /BLK1/A,B,C

COMMON Z,W,V /BLK1/D,E

are equivalent to the single statement

COMMON X,Y,Z,W,V /BLK1/A,B,C,D,E

## 6.9   ADDITIONAL SPECIFICATION STATEMENTS

Two specification statements which may prove useful in some problems are the EQUIVALENCE and DATA statements.

---

6.14 The EQUIVALENCE Statement

---

**EQUIVALENCE** (*a*1, *b*1, *c*1, . . .), (*a*2, *b*2, *c*2, . . .), . . .
where *a*1, *b*1, *c*1, . . . and *a*2, *b*2, *c*2, . . . are variable names.

---

Makes the variables within a set of parentheses all equivalent and representing the same storage location.

---

There are two motivating reasons for using equivalence statements:

1.  In a large program which is limited by memory size, several variables which do not overlap in use can be made equivalent, to save memory space.
2.  If the error of calling the same quantity by different names occurs in a program, it is safer and easier to correct by making different names equivalent, rather than by physically making all the names the same.

In the example

$$\text{EQUIVALENCE (X,Y,Z), (A,B)}$$

the variables X, Y, and Z are three names for the same quantity, just as A and B both represent another quantity.

---

6.15 The DATA Statement

---

**DATA** *A*1, *B*1, ... / *n* * *c*1, *n* * *d*1, ... / , *A*2, *B*2, ... / *n*
* *c*2, *n* * *d*2, ... /, ... where *A*1, *B*1, ... and A2, *B*2, ...
are variable names, *n* are repetition numbers, and *c*1, *d*1, ... and
*c*2, *d*2, ... are constants.

---

Specifies that the constants are to be stored in the corresponding
variables.

---

The DATA statement provides a method of initializing
variables to certain values without using arithmetic statements
during execution. The constants are defined during
compilation and loaded into the memory locations for the
respective variables. Thus no execution time is needed for
initialization of these variables. The DATA statement also
affords conservation of storage space, since the arithmetic
statements have been eliminated.

The following example

$$\text{DATA X,Y,Z/3.0,1.5,4.7/}$$

sets X = 3.0, Y = 1.5, and Z = 4.7.

The following example

$$\text{DATA A,B,C,D,E/3.5,3*1.0,2.4/}$$

sets A = 3.5, B, C, and D = 1.0, and E = 2.4.
If X is a subscripted variable of one dimension with a
maximum of 100 elements, the following example sets all
elements of X equal to zero.

$$\text{DATA X/100 *0.0/}$$

## 6.10 ARITHMETIC STATEMENT FUNCTIONS

Fortran IV provides a simple method of defining user-functions if the function is single valued and can be written with a single arithmetic statement. If these conditions are satisfied, the function can be defined within the calling program itself. No separate subprogram is involved. The only remaining requirement is that the defining statement must appear first in the program in which it is used or called. The standard way of writing the definition statement is given in Definition 6.16.

---

6.16 The Arithmetic Statement Function

---

*NAME (A,B,C, . . .) = E*
where *NAME* is any symbol (same as for subprograms), *A, B, C,* . . . are nonsubscripted variable names used as arguments, and *E* is any expression involving the arguments.

---

Defines a user-function called *NAME* with arguments *A, B, C,* . . . and equal to the value of the expression evaluated with the current values of the arguments. Calling procedures are the same as for supplied functions and function subprograms.

---

Figure 6.11 illustrates how an arithmetic function is defined and used.

The program in Figure 6.11 defines within it an arithmetic statement function called POLY. It has three arguments specified by the dummy variables A, B, and C. The expression to be evaluated for POLY is A*X**2+B*X+C, which is written in terms of the dummy variables A, B, and C as well as the variable X. The variables A, B, and C are considered independent from any other A, B, or C appearing

$$POLY(A,B,C) = A*X**2+B*X+C$$

.

.

$$A = 2*DATA$$
1  ALPHA = POLY(3.5,A,7.4)

.

.

2  BETA = ALPHA*POLY(P,Q,R) + 5.0

.

.

3  GAMMA = POLY(U+V,2*W,T/2)

.

.

END

**Figure 6.11  Arithmetic function.**

elsewhere in the program. However, the variable X within the function definition must be the same X appearing elsewhere in the program. Thus, the behavior of the program given above is as follows: Within statement numbered 1 a function call is made to the definition for POLY at the beginning of the program. The current values of the three dummy arguments are: A = 3.5, B = A, and C = 7.4. The second A here is independent from the first and represents a different value. The expression, A*X**2+B*X+C, is evaluated for these values of A, B, and C. The result is substituted into the expression of statement 1 which becomes the value of ALPHA. Statement numbered 2 actually causes the same effect as the following statement would:

$$BETA = ALPHA * (P*X**2+Q*X+R) + 5.0$$

Statement numbered 3 could be replaced by:

$$GAMMA = (U+V)*X**2+(2*W)*X+T/2$$

Thus, it is seen that the arithmetic statement function is a compromise between having no subprogram capability and using the function subprogram technique. The function is easier to use than the subprogram, but it has the limitation of allowing only one statement in the definition.

## PRACTICE EXERCISES

6.1 What is the difference between a main program and a subprogram, and which may be both a calling and a called program?

6.2 What must be rigorously guarded against in writing a series of subprogram calls? What is the proper name for this illegal operation?

6.3 Indicate distinct advantages of the function subprogram and the subroutine subprogram, respectively, which are not available with the other.

6.4 Explain why a variable name from the argument list of a function subprogram should not appear on the left-hand side of an equal sign within the subprogram, and why variable names from the main program, not in the argument list, may appear on the left of an equal sign in the subprogram.

6.5 In using function or subroutine subprograms, what conventions must be followed regarding the arguments in the calling sequence?

6.6 For a subroutine named HOUSE (I, J, K), with entries at Y(I, J, K) and Z(I, J, K), which of the following are valid call statements?

(a)  CALL HOUSE(I,J,K)      (c)  CALL Y(I,J,K)
(b)  CALL HOUSEY(I,J,K)    (d)  CALL YZ(I,J,K)

6.7 Write a function subprogram to evaluate the following single-valued function:

$$F(X) \;=\; \begin{cases} 5X - 1.0 & X \geq 0.0 \\ X^2 - 2X - 1.0 & X < 0.0 \end{cases}$$

6.8 Write a subroutine subprogram to compute the sum of each row of a 10 x 10 matrix. The first argument is the matrix name; the second argument is a vector of size 10 in which the answers are to be returned. The name of the subroutine is to be SUMS.

6.9  Indicate the purpose of each of the following:

(a)  EXTERNAL EXP, LOG

(b)  COMMON A, B, C

(c)  RETURN 2

(d)  EQUIVALENCE (X, Y, Z)

(e)  DATA A, B, C /1.5, 2*0.05/

(f)  ENTRY F(X, Y, Z)

6.10  What is the value of an arithmetic statement function, and where in the program must it appear?

# CHAPTER 7

# Logical, Complex, and Double-Precision Operations

## 7.1 INTRODUCTION

Until now, undivided attention has been given to the two basic modes of numbering, integer and real. Fortran IV, however, provides three additional modes of operation which have varying degrees of usefulness, beyond the needs of most basic programs. Presented in this chapter are the fundamental definitions, related operations, and Fortran IV statements concerned with logical, complex, and double-precision quantities.

Logical arithmetic is very useful in that most decision-making functions within a program can be reduced to simple true-false relationships. This mode of operation is applicable to almost any problem area or discipline.

Complex arithmetic, concerned with complex quantities and their operations, is generally restricted in its use to particular fields of endeavor such as electrical engineering or physics.

Double-precision arithmetic is very similar to the ordinary real-number operations discussed previously. The major differences lie in the accuracy of computations and the procedure for using double-precision quantities.

## 7.2 TYPE STATEMENTS

Unlike the names of real and integer variables, the names of the logical, complex, and double-precision variables must be defined as being one or the other through the use of type statements. Unless otherwise instructed, the Fortran IV compiler assumes that integer variable names begin with I, J, K, L, M, or N. Likewise, real variable names begin with letters other than I, J, K, L, M, or N. No letters have initially been allotted for logical, complex, or double-precision variable names. A method is provided, however, for changing this initial allocation to suit the needs of the programmer.

Before discussing *type* statements, a prerequisite point must be made. Each type of number (mode) requires a certain amount of storage space in the memory of the computer. There are also two sizes of storage space for each mode, a standard size and a nonstandard size. For example, integer numbers have two sizes, 2 and 4 units of storage. The 4 unit size is the standard size. The implication here is, if the corresponding values are relatively small, the programmer can save storage space by using the shorter form of integer number. Definition 7.1 shows all of the various sizes associated with the various modes of operation.

Continuing the discussion, type statements have two general forms, the explicit and the implicit. Explicit type statements define specific variable names as being one mode or another, while the implicit type statement changes the implied meaning of the first letter of variable names.

7.1 Storage Sizes or Lengths

| Mode | Standard size | Nonstandard size |
|---|---|---|
| INTEGER | 4 | 2 |
| REAL | 4 | $8^1$ |
| LOGICAL | 4 | 1 |
| COMPLEX | 8 | 16 |

[1]**REAL** * 8 is the same as double precision.

7.2 Explicit *TYPE* Statement

*TYPE* * *S* $V_1, V_2, V_3, \ldots$
where *TYPE* is either **INTEGER, REAL, LOGICAL,** or **COMPLEX,** * *S* is optional and is a size as specified in Definition 7.1, and $V_1, V_2, V_3, \ldots$ are variable names.

Defines $V_1, V_2, V_3, \ldots$ to be of the indicated mode with the indicated size.

**Examples:**

```
INTEGER X, ALPHA, K1
REAL * 8 R, SUM, DB2, J
LOGICAL * 4 P, Q, R
COMPLEX * 16 E, F, G, H
```

The first example shows three variable names, X, ALPHA, and K1, defined as integer variables with the standard length of 4 storage units. Note that normally K1 is integer anyway, however no harm is done by including it here. The second example defines the four variable names, R, SUM, DB2, and J as being REAL mode of 8 units length. This statement defines variables identical to those in the double-precision mode and could be specified by the following obsolete statement:

### DOUBLE PRECISION R, SUM, DB2, J

The third example defines P, Q, and R as logical variables of standard length. The fourth example defines E, F, G, and H as complex variable names of the nonstandard length of 16 units, sometimes referred to as complex double-precision quantities.

If the implied meaning of the first letter of a variable name is to be changed, the programmer uses an implicit type statement, shown in 7.3.

---

7.3 IMPLICIT *TYPE* Statement

---

**IMPLICIT** *TYPE* * S $(a_1, a_2, \ldots)$, *TYPE* * S $(a_1, a_2, \ldots)$, ...
where *TYPE* is **INTEGER, REAL, LOGICAL,** or **COMPLEX,** * S
is optional and indicates the size from Definition 7.1, and $a_1$,
$a_2, \ldots$ are either individual letters or a range of letters written as
$(a_1-a_2)$ where $a_1$ is the first and $a_2$ is the last letter of the range.

---

Changes the implied modal meaning of the first letter of the variable names used in the program.

---

**Example:**

IMPLICIT INTEGER * 2 (M—P), LOGICAL * 1 (A,B,C)

This example causes all variable names beginning with M, N, O, or P to be of INTEGER type with length 2. Names beginning with A, B, or C are to be LOGICAL with length 1. All other letters continue to have their standard meanings.

## 7.3  LOGICAL QUANTITIES AND OPERATIONS

Attention is now focused exclusively on the concept of logical quantities and operations.

A logical quantity is very simple to define, since a logical quantity may equal only two possible values, true or false.

| 7.4  Logical Constant |
| --- |
| **. TRUE . or . FALSE .** |
| A logical value that does not change during the course of computation. |

A logical quantity can be thought of as a switch which can either be ON or OFF. With the use of this concept, decision-making functions within a program can be reduced to simple true-false or yes-no relationships. To make the concept flexible, there must be logical quantities which can change during the course of computation. Therefore, a need exists for logical variable names to represent logical quantities, just as for integer and real variable names which represent integer and real quantities.

---

7.5 Logical Variables

---

Either:

1.  Symbols appearing in a logical type statement,
2.  Symbols beginning with a letter which appears in a logical implicit type statement.

---

Symbols which represent logical values which may change during the course of computation.

---

Before discussing logical expressions and statements, nine new operations are introduced and discussed. Three are called logical operators; six are called relational operators.

The three logical operators, .AND., .OR., and .NOT., are defined first.

---

7.6 The logical .AND. operation

---

**X .AND. Y**
where **X** and **Y** are any logical expressions.

|   |   | Y |   |
|---|---|---|---|
| .AND. | .FALSE. | .TRUE. |
| X .FALSE. | .FALSE. | .FALSE. |
| .TRUE. | .FALSE. | .TRUE. |

This is a truth table containing all possible values.

---

7.7 The logical .OR. operation

---

**X .OR. Y**
where **X** and **Y** are any logical expressions.

|          |  Y          |              |
|----------|-------------|--------------|
| .OR.     | .FALSE.     | .TRUE.       |
| X .FALSE.| .FALSE.     | .TRUE.       |
| .TRUE.   | .TRUE.      | .TRUE.       |

---

7.8 The logical .NOT. operation

---

**.NOT. X**
where **X** is any logical expression.

|       |  X        |          |
|-------|-----------|----------|
| .NOT. | .FALSE.   | .TRUE.   |
|       | .TRUE.    | .FALSE.  |

These logical operations apply only to logical operands and the results are always logical. The definitions of the relational operators appear next.

---

7.9  Relational Operators

---

**X .LT. Y**      Less than,
**X .LE. Y**      Less than or equal to,
**X .GT. Y**      Greater than,
**X .GE. Y**      Greater than or equal to,
**X .EQ. Y**      Equal to,
**X .NE. Y**      Not equal to,
where **X** and **Y** are any arithmetic expressions as defined in Chapter 2.

---

The result of any one of these operations is a logical value of true or false, depending on whether or not the values **X** and **Y** are related in the indicated way.

---

**Examples:**

X .LE. 5.4
A .GT. X + Y

Here the first example yields a result of true if the value of X is either less than or equal to 5.4, otherwise the result is false. Likewise, the second example is true if the value of A is greater than the sum of the two values, X and Y.

Perhaps it should be emphasized that the relational operators are actually a set of hybrid operators in that they are neither exclusively arithmetic nor exclusively logical. They involve arithmetic operands but their results are always logical, thus they actually transform arithmetic expressions into logical expressions. In this manner, the operators bridge the gap between the completely arithmetic and the totally logical expression.

## 7.4 LOGICAL EXPRESSIONS

At this point, a set of precise definitions and rules for forming logical expressions is presented. The definitions are similar to those given in Chapter 2 for arithmetic expressions and are parallel with them.

---

7.10 Logical Expression

---

Any valid combination of logical constants, variables, or functions, separated by logical operators; or arithmetic constants, variables, functions, or expressions separated by relational operators; or a combination of both.

---

Represents a logical thought.

---

Any logical constant or variable is a logical expression.

---

7.11 Rule 1 for Logical Expressions

---

7.12 Rule 2 for Logical Expressions

---

If **E** is a logical expression, then **.NOT. E** is a logical expression.

### 7.13 Rule 3 for Logical Expressions

If **E** is a logical expression, then **(E), ((E))**, and so on, are logical expressions.

### 7.14 Rule 4 for Logical Expressions

If **SMLFUN** is the name of some logical function of *n* variables, and if **E, F,...,H** are a set of *n* expressions, then **SMLFUN(E, F, . . . , H)** is a logical expression.

### 7.15 Rule 5 for Logical Expressions

If **E** and **F** are logical expressions, then **E .AND. F** and **E .OR. F** are logical expressions.

### 7.16 Rule 6 for Logical Expressions

If **E** and **F** are arithmetic expressions as given by definitions 2.21 through 2.26, then **E .LT. F, E .LE. F, E .GT. F, E .GE. F, E .EQ. F,** and **E .NE. F** are all logical expressions, in that the result is either true or false.

Just as arithmetic operations have certain hierarchy levels, so the logical and relational operations have associated hierarchy levels. To place all operations in proper perspective, a table is presented which defines the hierarchy for all operations available under Fortran IV. This table is an extension of Definition 2.28. Parenthetical expressions, function evaluation, and the assignment operator are also included to give a complete picture of all possible operations which can appear in arithmetic, assignment, and other statements.

---

**7.17 Complete Hierarchy Table for Operations**

1. Parenthetical expression evaluation(( . . . ))
2. Function evaluation **(F(X))**
3. Exponentiation **(\*\*)**
4. Multiplication and division (\* and /)
5. Addition and subtraction (+ and −)
6. Relational **(.LT., .LE., .GT., .GE., .EQ., .NE.)**
7. Logical not **(.NOT.)**
8. Logical and **(.AND.)**
9. Logical or **(.OR.)**
10. Assignment (=)

---

**Examples:**

1. A .AND. B
2. A .OR. .NOT. B
3. .NOT. A .OR. B .AND. C
4. .NOT. (A .OR. B .AND. C)
5. .NOT. ((A .OR. B) .AND. C)
6. X .GT. Y
7. X + 2.0 .LE. Y * Z
8. A .AND. X .EQ. Y

In these examples, assume that A, B, and C are all logical variables (that is, they appear in a logical type statement) and X, Y, and Z are ordinary real variables. The results of all eight examples are logical, either true or false.

The result of Example 1 is true if A and B are both true, otherwise false.

The result of Example 2 is false if A is false while B is true, otherwise true.

The result of Example 3 is true if A is false, or if B and C are both true, or both, otherwise false. In other words, the result is false if A is true while either B or C is false.

The result of Example 4 is true if A is false while either B or C is false, otherwise false. In other words, the result is false if A is true, or if B and C are both true, or both.

The result of Example 5 is true if C is false, or if A and B are both false, or both, otherwise false. In other words, the result is false if C is true while either A or B is true.

The result of Example 6 is true if the value of X is greater than Y, otherwise false.

The result of Example 7 is true if the value of X + 2.0 is less than or equal to the product of Y and Z.

The result of Example 8 is true if A is true while the values of X and Y are equal, otherwise it is false.

## 7.5 LOGICAL STATEMENTS

Fortran IV provides the programmer with two types of logical statements. A logical arithmetic statement, which computes logical quantities, is very much like the ordinary arithmetic statement used to compute integer or real quantities. The other statement is the logical IF, which is very useful in decision making.

---

**7.18** The Logical Arithmetic Statement

---

**A = B**

where **A** is any logical variable and **B** is any logical expression.

---

Causes the logical expression on the right to be computed and makes the variable on the left equal to the result.

---

**7.19** The Logical IF Statement

---

**IF** *(E)* *S*

where *E* is any logical expression and *S* is any statement except a DO, a logical IF, or a specification statement.

---

If the result of evaluating the expression, *E,* is true, then the statement, *S,* is executed. Otherwise, execution continues with the next statement in sequence.

---

As examples of how these two statements can be used, several variations of a program segment are shown for finding the largest element in a linear table of values. This example is the same as the problem illustrated in Section 5.5.

```
DIMENSION X(100)
LOGICAL A
      .
      .         statements defining X(I)
      .
BIG = X(1)
DO 1 I = 2, 100
A = BIG .GE. X(I)
IF(A) GO TO 1
BIG = X(I)
1 CONTINUE
      .
      .
      .
```

In this first variation, the variable A is defined as being logical. Within the DO loop, A is set to either true or false according to the relationship between the variable BIG and the Ith element of X. If BIG is greater than or equal to X(I), then A is true, otherwise false. The logical IF then tests the value of A. If A is true, the GO TO 1 statement is executed, thus skipping over the statement BIG = X(I). If A is false, the GO TO 1 statement is not executed and the next statement in sequence, BIG = X(I), is executed, making BIG equal to the largest X so far examined. A second variation is as follows:

```
DIMENSION X(100)
      .
      .         statements defining X(I)
      .
BIG = X(1)
DO 1 I = 2, 100
IF(BIG .GE. X(I)) GO TO 1
BIG = X(I)
1     CONTINUE
      .
      .
      .
```

In this example, the expression BIG .GE. X(I) is placed directly in the logical IF, rather than being equated to A. This method is easier and quicker, as long as the value of the expression is not needed for another purpose in the same DO loop. A third, even simpler version is now given:

```
DIMENSION X(100)
        .
        .           statements defining X(I)
        .
BIG = X(1)
DO 1 I = 2, 100
IF(BIG .LT. X(I)) BIG = X(I)
1    CONTINUE
        .
        .
        .
```

Here one can begin to see the power of the logical expression and the logical IF statement. By reversing the condition for truth or falsity, the BIG = X(I) statement is written directly within the logical IF and is executed or not on the same basis as before, in the other versions. Since logical IF statements can be used as the last statements in DO loops, the example can be further reduced to the following:

```
DIMENSION X(100)
        .
        .           statements defining X(I)
        .
BIG = X(1)
DO 1 I = 2, 100
1    IF(BIG .LT. X(I)) BIG = X(I)
        .
        .
        .
```

As a final example of logical operations, consider the hypothetical problem of reflection from the III quadrant into the I quadrant, and vice versa, of a two-dimensional space of variables $X$ and $Y$. In other words, when the values of $X$ and $Y$ are both positive or negative, the point thus represented is reflected through the origin into the opposite quadrant where the values of $X$ and $Y$ are the negative of their original values. This example clearly illustrates the power of relational operators in conjunction with logical operators.

```
     LOGICAL A
       .
       .    statements defining X and Y before reflection
       .
     A = X .LT. 0 .AND. Y .LT. 0 .OR. X . GT. 0 .AND. Y
   1 .GT. 0
     IF(A) X = −X
     IF(A) Y = −Y
       .
       .
       .
```

The value of A is true only if both X and Y are either both positive or both negative at the same time, otherwise A is false. Thus, in the two logical IF statements, the signs of X and Y are reversed only if A is true.

Input and output of logical data is accomplished with the L format field. The standard form is L$w$ where $w$ is the field width in columns.

On input, the variable associated with the field is set to true or false according to the first T or F read from the $w$ columns of the field, reading from left to right. If the entire field is blank or does not contain a T or F, the resulting value is false.

Output of a logical value causes either a letter T or a letter F to be written in the output field and to be right-adjusted with $w - 1$ leading blanks.

## 7.6 COMPLEX ARITHMETIC

It is assumed here that the reader is familiar with complex notation and operations. The essential thing the programmer needs to know about Fortran IV complex arithmetic is that each complex number stored and operated upon within the machine is kept as two real numbers, the first being the real part and the second being the imaginary part of the actual complex number. The steps which must be taken by the programmer are as follows. Complex constants are written in a special way, as is shown below. Either complex variables must be explicitly defined as such by an explicit type statement, or the first letter of the complex variable name must be implicitly defined as a complex variable letter by an implicit type statement (see Section 7.2). Input and output of complex data involves two real FORMAT fields, D, E, or F fields, for each complex number. Otherwise, no further effort is required by the programmer to specify complex arithmetic operations. The operations such as addition, subtraction, multiplication, and division of complex numbers are written no differently than the operations of ordinary real or integer numbers. The Fortran IV system automatically carries out complex arithmetic when complex numbers are encountered in expressions.

---

7.20 Complex Constant

---

$(C_1, C_2)$
where $C_1$ and $C_2$ are real constants as defined in Definition 2.13.

---

An ordered pair of real constants, the first being the real part, the second being the imaginary part of the desired complex constant. The constant does not change during the course of computation.

---

7.21 Complex Variable

---

Either:

1. Symbols appearing in an explicit complex type statement,
2. Symbols beginning with a letter which appears in an implicit complex type statement.

---

Represents complex quantities which may change during the course of computations.

---

A simple example of complex arithmetic is now given:

```
      COMPLEX A, B, C, D, X, Y
      READ (5, 1) X, Y
1     FORMAT (4F10.2)
      A = X + Y
      B = X − Y
      C = X * Y
      D = X / Y
      WRITE (6, 2) X, Y, A, B, C, D
2     FORMAT (12F10.2)
      STOP
      END
```

This program simply reads in two complex quantities, X and Y. Note that four real fields are needed. The complex sum, difference, product, and quotient are computed; the results are equated to A, B, C, and D, respectively. The input and the computed values are written out by the output device as X, Y, A, B, C, and D with each complex number requiring two real fields. Thus 12 real numbers appear on the output sheet.

Three useful supplied functions (See Appendix I for complete list) for complex arithmetic are:

1. REAL—obtains real part of complex argument,
2. AIMAG—obtains imaginary part of complex argument,
3. CMPLX—produces a complex number from two real arguments.

## 7.7 DOUBLE-PRECISION ARITHMETIC

Double-precision or real * 8 numbers provide more than twice the accuracy of ordinary real * 4 numbers. Real * 4 quantities maintain an accuracy between 6 and 7 decimal digits, while real * 8 values maintain between 16 and 17 decimal digits of accuracy. The programmer must remember, however, that double-precision operations usually require close to twice the computer time needed for single-precision operations; thus it is wise to exhaust all possible means to avoid using double-precision arithmetic. A programmer should investigate his techniques of solving a problem very carefully for any possible loss of accuracy before resorting to double-precision arithmetic.

---

7.22 Double-Precision Constant

---

A real constant written either with more than 7 decimal places or with a letter **D** in the place of the letter **E**.

---

Produces a constant with 17-place accuracy which does not change during the course of computation.

---

---

**7.23 Double-Precision Variable**

---

A symbol which either:
1. Appears in a **REAL * 8** explicit type statement,
2. Appears in a **DOUBLE PRECISION** type statement,
3. Begins with a letter appearing in an implicit **REAL * 8** type statement.

---

Represents a quantity with 17-place accuracy which may change during the course of computation.

---

Operations involving double-precision numbers are specified in the same way as ordinary real numbers. In fact, expressions may be written which involve integer * 2, integer * 4, real * 4, real * 8, complex * 8, and complex * 16 quantities. All computations are carried out in such a way that no loss of accuracy occurs. The operand hierarchy is now shown for all possible types of operands, an extension of Definition 2.30.

---

**7.24 Expression Operand Hierarchy**

---

1. Complex * 16
2. Complex * 8
3. Real * 8
4. Real * 4
5. Integer * 4
6. Integer * 2

## 7.8 FORTRAN IV OPERATION SUMMARY

In order to give a complete, yet brief description of all possible valid operations, Tables I through V are given.

Table I shows all valid operands for the +, —, *, and / operators and the type of quantity for the result. Operands are shown at the left-hand side and at the top of the table, with the result shown at the intersection of a given row and column.

Table II shows valid combinations of operands and results for the operator **. Operands are shown as in Table I except that the table is not symmetric. In A**B, A is shown at the left-hand side and B is shown at the top of the table.

Table III shows all valid operands for the relational operators, .LT., .LE., .GT., .GE., .EQ., and .NE.

Table IV shows all valid operands for the operators, .AND., .OR., and .NOT.

Finally, Table V shows all valid left- and right-hand sides of the assignment operator, =, and the resulting type. In A = B, A is shown at the left-hand side and B is shown at the top of the table.

*TABLE I*

| + − * / | Integer 2 | Integer 4 | Real 4 | Real 8 | Complex 8 | Complex 16 |
|---|---|---|---|---|---|---|
| Integer 2 | Integer 2 | Integer 4 | Real 4 | Real 8 | Complex 8 | Complex 16 |
| Integer 4 | Integer 4 | Integer 4 | Real 4 | Real 8 | Complex 8 | Complex 16 |
| Real 4 | Real 4 | Real 4 | Real 4 | Real 8 | Complex 8 | Complex 16 |
| Real 8 | Real 8 | Real 8 | Real 8 | Real 8 | Complex 8 | Complex 16 |
| Complex 8 | Complex 8 | Complex 8 | Complex 8 | Complex 8 | Complex 8 | Complex 16 |
| Complex 16 | Complex 16 | Complex 16 | Complex 16 | Complex 16 | Complex 16 | Complex 16 |

*TABLE II*

| ** | Integer 2 | Integer 4 | Real 4 | Real 8 | Complex 8 | Complex 16 |
|---|---|---|---|---|---|---|
| Integer 2 | Integer 2 | Integer 4 | Real 4 | Real 8 | | |
| Integer 4 | Integer 4 | Integer 4 | Real 4 | Real 8 | | |
| Real 4 | Real 4 | Real 4 | Real 4 | Real 8 | | |
| Real 8 | Real 8 | Real 8 | Real 8 | Real 8 | | |
| Complex 8 | Complex 8 | Complex 8 | | | | |
| Complex 16 | Complex 16 | Complex 16 | | | | |

*TABLE III*

| .LT. .LE. .GT. .GE. .NE. .EQ. | Integer 2 | Integer 4 | Real 4 | Real 8 |
|---|---|---|---|---|
| Integer 2 | Logical | Logical | Logical | Logical |
| Integer 4 | Logical | Logical | Logical | Logical |
| Real 4 | Logical | Logical | Logical | Logical |
| Real 8 | Logical | Logical | Logical | Logical |

*TABLE IV*

| .AND. .OR. .NOT.[1] | Logical 1 | Logical 4 |
|---|---|---|
| Logical 1 | Logical 1 | Logical 4 |
| Logical 4 | Logical 4 | Logical 4 |

[1] NOT. is a unary operator; therefore, use one row or one column.

*TABLE V*

| A = B<br>A | Integer<br>2 | Integer<br>4 | Real<br>4 | Real<br>8 | Complex<br>8 | Complex<br>16 | Logical<br>1 | Logical<br>4 |
|---|---|---|---|---|---|---|---|---|
| Integer<br>2 | Integer<br>2 | Integer<br>2 | Integer<br>2 | Integer<br>2 | Integer<br>2 | Integer<br>2 | | |
| Integer<br>4 | Integer<br>4 | Integer<br>4 | Integer<br>4 | Integer<br>4 | Integer<br>4 | Integer<br>4 | | |
| Real<br>4 | Real<br>4 | Real<br>4 | Real<br>4 | Real<br>4 | Real<br>4 | Real<br>4 | | |
| Real<br>8 | Real<br>8 | Real<br>8 | Real<br>8 | Real<br>8 | Real<br>8 | Real<br>8 | | |
| Complex<br>8 | Complex<br>8 | Complex<br>8 | Complex<br>8 | Complex<br>8 | Complex<br>8 | Complex<br>8 | | |
| Complex<br>16 | Complex<br>16 | Complex<br>16 | Complex<br>16 | Complex<br>16 | Complex<br>16 | Complex<br>16 | | |
| Logical<br>1 | | | | | | | Logical<br>1 | Logical<br>1 |
| Logical<br>4 | | | | | | | Logical<br>4 | Logical<br>4 |

## PRACTICE EXERCISES

7.1 Write explicit type statements to define:

(a) X, Y, and Z to be complex of size 16;

(b) A, B, DATA, LINE, and MATRIX to be real of size 8;

(c) P1, P2, Q1, Q2, R1, and R2 to be integer of size 2;

(d) ITEM1, ITEM2, and ITEM3 to be real of size 4;

(e) L, LL, M, and MM to be logical of size 4.

7.2 Write one implicit type statement defining:

(a) A through E to be real of size 8,

(b) I through K to be integer of size 2,

(c) P through R to be logical of size 1,

(d) X through Z to be complex of size 16,

(e) U through W to be complex of size 8.

7.3 Write a single statement that will double X if X is greater than 5.0.

7.4 Write a logical expression that will be true only if both X and Y are equal and A is less than B.

7.5 Write a logical expression that will be true if either X is less than 1.5 or Y is equal to 10.0.

7.6 Write a statement that will branch to statement 25 if the condition in Problem 7.4 is not true.

7.7 Using logical variables, logical assignment statements, and a logical IF, set A = B + C if the conditions in Problems 7.4 and 7.5 both are true.

7.8 Assuming X and Y are complex variables, indicate how X can be set equal to Y plus the complex number, 2 + i5.

7.9 Using the REAL, AIMAG, and CMPLX supplied functions together with real and complex variables, show how to obtain the conjugate of a complex number. This operation is actually provided by the CONJG supplied function.

7.10 From Table I, determine what type of quantities are invalid operands for the operators +, −, *, and /.

7.11 From Table II, determine what type of quantities are invalid operands for the operator **.

7.12 From Table III, determine what type of quantities are invalid operands for the relational operators.

7.13 From Table IV, determine what type of quantities are invalid operands for the logical operators.

7.14 From Table V, determine what combinations of left- and right-hand sides of the = sign are invalid.

CHAPTER **8**

# Sequential and Direct Access Storage Operations

## 8.1 INTRODUCTION

In this concluding chapter, the subject of storage devices, their characteristics, and the use of them with Fortran IV, will be presented. In modern computer usage, many special situations can arise where unusual storage requirements exist. For example, data can be obtained concerning a problem at hand that must be manipulated by several different programs. Perhaps output from one program becomes input to a second program, and so forth. This type of data-handling problem usually becomes much easier if magnetic tape is used instead of cards for storage, input, and output purposes. A second type of data-handling problem exists when elements in a very large data file need to be retrieved or updated in a random fashion. Such a problem usually becomes feasible only when disk storage is used for the data file. Therefore, the purpose of this chapter is first to describe typical storage devices and indicate their advantages and disadvantages. The Fortran IV statements needed to use these devices will then be described and illustrated.

## 8.2 STORAGE DEVICES AND THEIR CHARACTERISTICS

There are many different types, sizes, and speeds of storage devices, most of which can be placed into one of three categories. The choice of the category is based on how the computer stores or retrieves data in the device. This process is referred to as access, which is sequential, direct, or random in nature. The type of access is a consequence of the physical design and organization of the device which, in turn, is based on a trade-off between access speed and cost.

---

8.1 Random Access Storage

---

Random access storage is characterized by an access time or speed which is independent of where in the data file the desired data item is located.

---

Stated in another way, one piece of data is just as accessible as any other piece of data in terms of the time needed to access that data. Most main storage units of computers are of this type. Due to the large cost factor involved, the amount of main storage capacity is quite limited. Even the largest computers are held to a storage size on the order of one million bytes. A byte is a number, eight binary bits in length, and is the same size as a storage unit, which was discussed in Definition 7.1. Thus a standard size integer or real number requires four bytes.

8.2 Direct Access Storage

Direct access storage is characterized by an access time or speed which is somewhat dependent on where in the data file the desired data item is located.

Putting it another way, one piece of data is not as accessible as any other piece of data in terms of the time needed to access that data. This type of device is typified by disk, drum, and data cell storage units. All of these devices depend on moving magnetic surfaces on which data is recorded. Since access is usually made through a fixed read/write head, a rotational delay is experienced during an attempt to reach a particular data item. The major concept is to endure relatively short and tolerable delays, while providing much larger storage capacities, usually 10–100 million bytes, and still allow reasonable access to any data within the entire file.

8.3 Sequential Access Storage

Sequential access storage is characterized by an access time or speed which is totally dependent on where in the data file the desired data item is located.

Stated differently, one piece of data is definitely not as accessible as any other piece of data in terms of the time needed to access that data. This type of device is represented by tape drives, card readers and punches, printers, and typewriter keyboards. To reach an item of data in these devices, access must be made through all the data between the starting point of access and the item itself. The advantage of this type of device is the relatively low cost for an essentially unlimited storage capacity. Such economy consequently results in the sacrifice of high access speeds.

No special Fortran IV feature is required to use random access main storage, since all programs normally reside there anyway. Nevertheless it should now be obvious why all good programmers go to extremes to limit the size of a program as well as its data files to fit into main storage and to thereby take full advantage of its access speed.

Sections are now presented describing the need for and the techniques of using sequential and direct access storage facilities through special Fortran IV language features.

## 8.3  SEQUENTIAL ACCESS APPLICATIONS

Since the purposes and uses of the card reader, card punch, and printer were discussed in Chapter 4, this section is limited to the discussion of magnetic tape, its applications and its advantages.

*As primary input:* Masses of data can be transferred from cards to tape by a less expensive machine than the one which processes the data. The tape then makes a faster, more reliable, and more convenient means of supplying input to the main processor.

In certain data-gathering applications, a direct keyboard to a magnetic tape device might prove more effective than card punching.

Some data-acquisition systems produce magnetic tape records directly, for use on another computer as primary input.

In certain extremely large data-gathering situations, a national census, for instance, special equipment may be used to transfer data from one medium to another, such as from microfilm to magnetic tape.

*As primary output:* Output data can be written on magnetic tape for later printing on a less expensive machine than the main processor. This practice also provides a convenient way of keeping the data for contingency purposes.

Magnetic tape is a fairly convenient medium for shipping data from one geographical location to another.

*As semipermanent or permanent storage:* Output data, which later becomes input data to another processing stage, can be saved conveniently on magnetic tape. However, if the time between runs gets very small or if the access must be random rather than sequential, a more expensive method of storage may be necessary.

Magnetic tape is particularly effective in business applications involving periodic processing of payroll, inventory, or account records.

## 8.4 SEQUENTIAL ACCESS TECHNIQUES FOR MAGNETIC TAPE

The READ and WRITE statements presented in Chapter 4 are also applicable to the use of magnetic tape. However, several details were not discussed at that time. Therefore, these statements are defined more completely in this section. At the same time, the concept of "end of file" (EOF) processing and error detection is introduced.

---

8.4 READ Statement

---

**READ** *(a, b,* END = *c*, ERR = *d) list*
where *a* is either an unsigned integer constant or integer variable of size 4, *b* is optional and is either a FORMAT statement number or an array name which contains a FORMAT, *c* is optional and is a statement number to be transferred to upon encountering the "end of file" (EOF) or end of the data set, *d* is optional and is a statement number to be transferred to upon encountering an error condition during reading, *list* is optional and is a series of variable or array names, separated by commas.

---

Specifies that data for the variables in the list are to be read from unit *a* using FORMAT *b* as a guide. Upon detection of (1) end of file, go to statement *c;* (2) error condition, go to statement *d*. If *c* or *d* are needed and are missing, the program terminates execution.

Ignoring the end of file and error condition options, the following general forms of the READ statement can be written:

| | |
|---|---|
| READ *(a, b)* list | where *a* and *b* are integer |
| READ *(N, b)* list | constants. N is an integer |
| READ *(a, X)* list | variable. X is an array name. |
| READ (N, X) *list* | |

In addition, each of these statements could be written without the list as well as without the format indication, thus making a total of 16 forms.

The unit number *a*, or that represented by N, is usually preset at a given installation for the card reader, punch, and printer. For example, the unit number

5 usually refers to the card reader,
6 usually refers to the line printer,
7 usually refers to the card punch.

Some other unit number usually must be assigned by the user for magnetic tape units, in conjunction with local computing center rules and regulations. Usually this number can be assigned by inserting a special control card into the program card deck. Some centers have permanent unit numbers preassigned for specific uses.

When magnetic tape is used with a FORMAT statement, the data must be written on the tape in an external alphanumeric mode much like card code. Reading data from magnetic tape resembles reading data from cards or pseudocards except in record lengths, which are not restricted to 80 columns as in real cards. In every other way, formatting considerations are identical.

**Example:**

READ (2, 17) (X(I), I = 1, 50)

This statement reads 50 numbers for X(I) from unit 2 using FORMAT statement 17 as a guide. The behavior is very similar to reading data from cards.

When magnetic tape is used without a FORMAT statement, the data must be written in an internal mode, which usually means that the tape was originally written by a corresponding unformatted WRITE statement. The major reason for using this mode of operation is the higher speed of transcription which is obtained. The main point to be understood about this mode of operation is the meaning of a record. A single record is produced by a single execution of a WRITE statement. Therefore, the READ statement list should usually correspond to the WRITE statement list if the records are to be of compatible size. If a READ list is shorter than the record being read, the tape stops at the actual end of the record, not the middle. If the list is longer, enough records are read to supply the demand, but again the tape stops at the end of the current record. Thus, subsequent reads always begin with a new record in either situation.

**Example:**

> READ (3, END = 10) (A(1, J), J = 1, 10)

Here data for A(1, J) is read from unit 3 without the use of a FORMAT statement. In case the end of file mark is encountered during reading, transfer is made to statement 10.

---

8.5 WRITE Statement

---

**WRITE** *(a, b) list*
where *a, b* and *list* are as in the READ statement. End of file and error exits cannot be specified.

---

Specifies that the data associated with the list variables will be written on unit *a* using FORMAT *b* as a guide.

---

Variations of the WRITE statement can be given as was done for the READ. Similar remarks can be made about their use with the obvious change in the direction of data transfer.

**Examples:**

WRITE (2, 17) (X(I), I = 1, 50)
WRITE (3) (A(1, J), J = 1, 10)

These two WRITE statements would write records with the same formats as the two previous READ statement examples.

In addition to READ and WRITE statements, three additional Fortran IV statements are provided which are useful in magnetic tape operations. These are the REWIND, END FILE, and BACKSPACE.

---

8.6 REWIND Statement

---

**REWIND** *a*
where *a* is either an unsigned integer constant or an integer variable.

---

Specifies that the tape on unit *a* is to be rewound to its beginning or load point for subsequent reading, writing, or unloading.

---

8.7 END FILE Statement

---

**END FILE** *a*
where *a* is either an unsigned integer constant or an integer variable.

---

Specifies that the tape on unit *a* is to have an end of file mark recorded, thus producing a logical end to a group of records just written.

---

8.8 BACKSPACE Statement

---

**BACKSPACE** *a*
where *a* is either an unsigned integer constant or an integer variable.

---

Specifies that the tape on unit *a* is to be backspaced one record.

---

The purpose of the END FILE statement is to provide the programmer a means of placing a machine-sensible recording on the tape at the logical end of a sequence of records. This mark provides a machine-sensible indicator that can be detected when the tape is read at a later date. This indicator is highly useful when prior knowledge of the number of records on the tape is not known.

The purpose of the REWIND and BACKSPACE statements is to provide means of repositioning the tape at any time during the process of reading or writing. To position in the forward direction without reading, one must use a READ statement either without a list or with a dummy list.

## 8.5 DIRECT ACCESS TECHNIQUES AND APPLICATIONS

Direct access storage devices become very useful in problems that involve large sets of data and that require nonsequential or direct access.

Four special statements are provided for use with direct access storage. One, the DEFINE FILE statement, must always be used to specify those direct access files which are to be used during the execution of a program. DEFINE FILE is a specification statement similar to the DIMENSION statement; either of which must appear within the program before the respective files or variables are used. In addition, special READ and WRITE statements are also provided for direct access data files. The final statement is the FIND statement which can be used to preceed a READ. Between them may appear computation statements, thus allowing overlap of input with computation.

---

### 8.9 DEFINE FILE Statement

---

**DEFINE FILE** $a_1$ $(m_1, r_1, f_1, v_1)$, $a_2$ $(m_2, r_2, f_2, v_2)$, . . .
where $a$, $m$, and $r$ are integer constants, $f$ is either an L, E, or U, and $v$ is an unsubscripted integer variable.

---

Specifies a set of direct access data files with reference numbers $a_i$, containing $m_i$ records, with a record size of $r_i$, formatting indicated by $f_i =$

(1)   L with or without FORMAT control, record size $r_i$ measured in storage locations;

(2)   E with FORMAT control, $r_i$ measured in storage locations or characters;

(3)   U without FORMAT control, $r_i$ measured in storage words (a word is equal to storage locations divided by 4, rounded up to nearest integer);

and $v_i$ is an associated variable which points to the next record after a READ or WRITE, or the record found by a FIND.

---

**Example:**

DEFINE FILE 2(50,100,L,I2), 3(100,50,E,J)

This statement defines two direct access data files: The first, with reference number 2, has 50 records, each containing 100 storage locations or characters, with an associated variable I2. A FORMAT may or may not be used. The second file has reference number 3, containing 100 records, each containing 50 characters, with associated variable J. A FORMAT must be used.

The number of storage locations required by a set of variables can be determined by adding up the various sizes of each variable as specified in Chapter 7, Definition 7.1. Normally, one storage location is required for a single character, as described in Chapter 4 regarding the A field specification.

In addition to the DEFINE FILE statement, an additional control card for each direct access data file must normally be included in the program card deck, as specified by local computing center rules.

---

8.10 Direct Access READ Statement

---

**READ** *(a'r, b,* ERR *= d) list*
where *a* is an integer constant or variable, *r* is any integer expression, *b* is an optional FORMAT statement number, *d* is a statement number, and *list* is a list of variables.

---

Causes data to be read from record *r* within direct access data file *a*. If *b* is specified, the indicated FORMAT statement is used for FORMAT control. If an error is detected during input, transfer is made to statement number *d*.

---

**Example:**

$$\text{READ (2'I,5,ERR=6) (X(K), K=1,10)}$$

This statement causes 10 values to be read from direct access data set number 2 beginning with record number I. FORMAT statement number 5 is used for FORMAT control. If an error is detected, statement number 6 receives control.

8.11 Direct Access WRITE Statement

---

**WRITE** *(a'r, b) list*
where *a* is an integer constant or variable, *r* is an integer expression, *b* is an optional FORMAT statement number, and *list* is a list of variables.

---

Causes data for the list of variables to be written into direct access data file *a* beginning with record *r*. If *b* is given, statement number *b* is used for FORMAT control.

**Example:**

# WRITE (4'J+2) X, Y, Z

This statement causes the values of X, Y, and Z to be written into record J+2 of direct access data file number 4. No FORMAT statement is specified.

8.12 Direct Access FIND Statement

---

**FIND** *(a'r)*
where *a* is an integer constant or variable and *r* is an integer expression.

---

Causes record *r* of direct access data file *a* to be located for a subsequent READ operation. Computations may proceed during the **FIND** operation.

To conclude this chapter, the following example of direct access utilization is presented.

```
      DIMENSION NAME(5)
      DEFINE FILE 10(7500, 42, E, IASSOC)
50    READ (9, 2) ID, PRCHSE
 2    FORMAT(I4, F6.2)
      READ (10'ID,3) SBAL, CBAL
 3    FORMAT(T25, F9.2, F9.2)
      IF(CBAL .LT. PRCHSE) GO TO 6
 4    WRITE (9, 5)
 5    FORMAT('** PURCHASE OK **')
      CBAL = CBAL − PRCHSE
      GO TO 9
 6    IF(SBAL .LT. PRCHSE) GO TO 7
      WRITE (9, 5)
      SBAL = SBAL − PRCHSE
      GO TO 9
 7    WRITE (9, 8)
 8    FORMAT('** PURCHASE NOT OK **')
      GO TO 50
 9    READ (10'ID, 10) ID, NAME
10    FORMAT(I4, 5A4, 2F9.2)
      WRITE (10'ID, 10) ID, NAME, SBAL, CBAL
      GO TO 50
      STOP
      END
```

This program could be used by a banking organization to allow real time checking of customer account balances, as a service to retail merchants. Assume the bank has 7500 customers, each having an ID number between 1 and 7500. This ID number would identify an account record in a direct access data file within the bank's computing system. Each account record has the following format:

| Columns | Field | Type |
|---------|-------|------|
| 1 − 4 | Customer ID | I4 |
| 5 − 24 | Customer name | 5A4 |
| 25 − 33 | Savings balance | F9.2 |
| 34 − 42 | Checking balance | F9.2 |

When a purchase is being made, the store clerk enters into a simple terminal device the customer's ID number and the amount of purchase. These values are read by statement numbered 50 in the program. Unit 9 here is the number of the remote terminal. With the use of the customer's ID number, the present account balances are read from the direct access data file, SBAL and CBAL. The program checks to see if the purchase amount is less than the amount in either the checking or savings accounts. If so, the amount of the purchase is subtracted from the account and the balance is updated with the direct access WRITE statement. Notice that in order to rewrite the record, the entire record must be rewritten, thus the NAME is read by the direct access READ statement numbered 9, before the update occurs. If the amount of the purchase is greater than the amount on balance, a message saying '** PURCHASE NOT OK **' is sent back to the store, otherwise the message '** PURCHASE OK **' is returned.

In this application it is easy to see the advantage of the direct access technique of data input, output, and storage.

## PRACTICE EXERCISES

8.1 Describe the three types of storage devices presented in Section 8.2. Explain the differences between capacities and costs.

8.2 Write a READ statement that will read data for two arrays, X(100) and A(10, 10), from tape unit 3. FORMAT statement number 6 matches the data fields. In case of an end of file condition, transfer to statement 10 should be made. An error condition should cause statement 20 to be executed next.

8.3 Write a WRITE statement that will produce a single record of internal code (FORMAT statement not used) on unit 1 for the following arrays: A(10, 10), B(1000), C(3, 4, 5).

8.4 If several related records have been written using the statement of Problem 8.3 and are to be segregated from subsequent data, what action should be taken?

8.5 What statement should be used to
   (a) Reposition a tape to completely reread it?
   (b) Reposition a tape to reread the last record read?
   (c) Skip records on a tape?

8.6 Provide a DEFINE FILE statement that will set up three direct access files as follows:
   (a) Reference number 1, to have 500 records of 10 characters each, to be formatted, and to have an associated variable of I1.
   (b) Reference 2, to have 200 records requiring 100 storage locations each, not to be formatted, and to have an associated variable of I2.
   (c) Reference 3, to have 300 records requiring 80 storage locations each, may be formatted, and to have I3 as the associated variable.

8.7 Using a file specified by Exercise 8.6, write READ and FORMAT statements to read a record specified by the expression, K + 3, from file number 1. The field specifications for a record are 2F5.2. The variables being read are A and B. If an error is detected, transfer to statement 15.

8.8 How could one easily read the very next record after the one read by Problem 8.7?

8.9 Write a WRITE statement to write a record into file 2 (Problem 8.6), record I2. The variables being written are: X(I), $1 \leq I \leq 20$, Y(J), $1 \leq J \leq 5$.

8.10 Write a FIND statement to locate record K + M in file 3 of Problem 8.6.

# Fortran IV
# Supplied Functions

Column Legends:
    A, in-line (I) or out-of-line (0);
    B, number of arguments;
    C, type of arguments;
    D, type of function value.

| Function | Entry name | Definition | A | B | C | D |
|---|---|---|---|---|---|---|
| Exponential | EXP | $e^{arg}$ | 0 | 1 | R * 4 | R * 4 |
|  | DEXP | $e^{arg}$ | 0 | 1 | R * 8 | R * 8 |
|  | CEXP | $e^{arg}$ | 0 | 1 | C * 8 | C * 8 |
|  | CDEXP | $e^{arg}$ | 0 | 1 | C * 16 | C * 16 |
| Natural logarithm | ALOG | $\ln(arg)$ | 0 | 1 | R * 4 | R * 4 |
|  | DLOG | $\ln(arg)$ | 0 | 1 | R * 8 | R * 8 |
|  | CLOG | $\ln(arg)$ | 0 | 1 | C * 8 | C * 8 |
|  | CDLOG | $\ln(arg)$ | 0 | 1 | C * 16 | C * 16 |
| Common logarithm | ALOG10 | $\log_{10}(arg)$ | 0 | 1 | R * 4 | R * 4 |
|  | ALOG10 | $\log_{10}(arg)$ | 0 | 1 | R * 8 | R * 8 |
| Arc sine | ARSIN | $\arcsin(arg)$ | 0 | 1 | R * 4 | R * 4 |
|  | DARSIN | $\arcsin(arg)$ | 0 | 1 | R * 8 | R * 8 |

| Function | Entry name | Definition | A | B | C | D |
|---|---|---|---|---|---|---|
| Arc cosine | ARCOS | arccos(arg) | 0 | 1 | R * 4 | R * 4 |
| | DARCOS | arccos(arg) | 0 | 1 | R * 8 | R * 8 |
| Arc tangent | ATAN | arctan(arg) | 0 | 1 | R * 4 | R * 4 |
| | ATAN2 | arctan(arg$_1$/arg$_2$) | 0 | 2 | R * 4 | R * 4 |
| | DATAN | arctan(arg) | 0 | 1 | R * 8 | R * 8 |
| | DATAN2 | arctan(arg$_1$/arg$_2$) | 0 | 2 | R * 8 | R * 8 |
| Trigonometric sine (argument in radians) | SIN | sin(arg) | 0 | 1 | R * 4 | R * 4 |
| | DSIN | sin(arg) | 0 | 1 | R * 8 | R * 8 |
| | CSIN | sin(arg) | 0 | 1 | C * 8 | C * 8 |
| | CDSIN | sin(arg) | 0 | 1 | C * 16 | C * 16 |
| Trigonometric cosine (argument in radians) | COS | cos(arg) | 0 | 1 | R * 4 | R * 4 |
| | DCOS | cos(arg) | 0 | 1 | R * 8 | R * 8 |
| | CCOS | cos(arg) | 0 | 1 | C * 8 | C * 8 |
| | CDCOS | cos(arg) | 0 | 1 | C * 16 | C * 16 |
| Trigonometric tangent (argument in radians) | TAN | tan(arg) | 0 | 1 | R * 4 | R * 4 |
| | DTAN | tan(arg) | 0 | 1 | R * 8 | R * 8 |
| Trigonometric cotangent (argument in radians) | COTAN | cotan(arg) | 0 | 1 | R * 4 | R * 4 |
| | DCOTAN | cotan(arg) | 0 | 1 | R * 8 | R * 8 |
| Square root | SQRT | (arg)$^{1/2}$ | 0 | 1 | R * 4 | R * 4 |
| | DSQRT | (arg)$^{1/2}$ | 0 | 1 | R * 8 | R * 8 |
| | CSQRT | (arg)$^{1/2}$ | 0 | 1 | C * 8 | C * 8 |
| | CDSQRT | (arg)$^{1/2}$ | 0 | 1 | C * 16 | C * 16 |
| Hyperbolic tangent | TANH | tanh(arg) | 0 | 1 | R * 4 | R * 4 |
| | DTANH | tanh(arg) | 0 | 1 | R * 16 | R * 16 |
| Hyperbolic sine | SINH | sinh(arg) | 0 | 1 | R * 4 | R * 4 |
| | DSINH | sinh(arg) | 0 | 1 | R * 8 | R * 8 |
| Hyperbolic cosine | COSH | cosh(arg) | 0 | 1 | R * 4 | R * 4 |
| | DCOSH | cosh(arg) | 0 | 1 | R * 8 | R * 8 |
| Error fnctn | ERF | $(2/\pi) \int_0^x e^{-u^2} du$ | 0 | 1 | R * 4 | R * 4 |
| | DERF | | 0 | 1 | R * 8 | R * 8 |
| Complemented error fnctn | ERFC | $1 - erf(x)$ | 0 | 1 | R * 4 | R * 4 |
| | DERFC | | 0 | 1 | R * 8 | R * 8 |

| Function | Entry name | Definition | A | B | C | D |
|---|---|---|---|---|---|---|
| Gamma | GAMMA | $\int_0^\infty u^{x-1}e^{-u}du$ | 0 | 1 | R * 4 | R * 4 |
|  | DGAMMA |  | 0 | 1 | R * 8 | R * 8 |
| Log Gamma | ALGAMA | $\text{Ln }\Gamma(x)$ | 0 | 1 | R * 4 | R * 4 |
|  | DLGAMA |  | 0 | 1 | R * 8 | R * 8 |
| Modular arithmetic | MOD | $\arg_1(\text{mod }\arg_2)=$ $\arg_1-(x)*\arg_2$ Where: $(x)$ is the largest integer whose magnitude does not exceed the magnitude of $\arg_1/\arg_2$. The sign of the integer is the same as the sign of $\arg_1/\arg_2$. | I | 2 | I * 4 | I * 4 |
|  | AMOD |  | I | 2 | R * 4 | R * 4 |
|  | DMOD |  | I | 2 | R * 8 | R * 8 |
| Absolute value | IABS | $\lvert\,\text{arg}\,\rvert$ | I | 1 | I * 4 | I * 4 |
|  | ABS |  | I | 1 | R * 4 | R * 4 |
|  | DABS |  | I | 1 | R * 8 | R * 8 |
|  | CABS | $(a^2+b^2)$ for $a+bi$ | 0 | 1 | C * 8 | C * 8 |
|  | CDABS |  | 0 | 1 | C * 16 | C * 16 |
| Truncation | INT | Sign of arg times largest integer $\leq\lvert\,\text{arg}\,\rvert$ | I | 1 | R * 4 | I * 4 |
|  |  |  | I | 1 | R * 4 | R * 4 |
|  | AINT |  | I | 1 | R * 4 | R * 4 |
|  | IDINT |  | I | 1 | R * 8 | I * 4 |
| Largest value | AMAX0 | $\text{Max}(\arg_1, \arg_2, \cdots)$ | 0 | $\geq 2$ | I * 4 | R * 4 |
|  | AMAX1 |  | 0 | $\geq 2$ | R * 4 | R * 4 |
|  | MAX0 |  | 0 | $\geq 2$ | I * 4 | I * 4 |
|  | MAX1 |  | 0 | $\geq 2$ | R * 4 | I * 4 |
|  | DMAX1 |  | 0 | $\geq 2$ | R * 8 | R * 8 |
| Smallest[1] value | AMIN0 | $\text{Min}(\arg_1, \arg_2, \cdots)$ | 0 | $\geq 2$ | I * 4 | R * 4 |
|  | AMIN1 |  | 0 | $\geq 2$ | R * 4 | R * 4 |
|  | MIN0 |  | 0 | $\geq 2$ | I * 4 | I * 4 |
|  | MIN1 |  | 0 | $\geq 2$ | R * 4 | I * 4 |
|  | DMIN1 |  | 0 | $\geq 2$ | R * 8 | R * 8 |
| Float | FLOAT | Convert from integer to real | I | 1 | I * 4 | R * 4 |
|  | DFLOAT |  | I | 1 | I * 4 | R * 8 |

[1] For the Fortran IV (H) compiler, these functions are in-line.

| Function | Entry name | Definition | A | B | C | D |
|---|---|---|---|---|---|---|
| Fix | IFIX | Convert from | I | 1 | R * 4 | I * 4 |
|  | HFIX | real to integer | I | 1 | R * 4 | I * 2 |
| Transfer of sign | SIGN | Sign of $\text{arg}_2 \times$ $\mid \text{arg}_1 \mid$ | I | 2 | R * 4 | R * 4 |
|  | ISIGN |  | I | 2 | I * 4 | I * 4 |
|  | DSIGN |  | I | 2 | R * 8 | R * 8 |
| Positive difference | DIM | $\text{arg}_1 - \text{Min}(\text{arg}_1,$ $\text{arg}_2)$ | I | 2 | R * 4 | R * 4 |
|  | IDIM |  | I | 2 | I * 4 | I * 4 |
| Obtaining most signif- icant part of a real * 8 argument | SNGL |  | I | 1 | R * 8 | R * 4 |
| Obtain real part of com- plex argument | REAL |  | I | 1 | C * 8 | R * 4 |
| Obtain imaginary part of com- plex argument | AIMAG |  | I | 1 | C * 8 | R * 4 |
| Express a real * 4 argmnt in R * 8 form | DBLE |  | I | 1 | R * 4 | R * 8 |
| Express two real argmnts in complex form | CMPLX | $C = \text{arg}_1 + \text{arg}_2$ | I | 2 | R * 4 | C * 8 |
| Obtain con- jugate of a complex argument | CONJG | $C = X - iY$ | I | 1 | C * 8 | C * 8 |
|  | DCONJG | For arg $= X + iY$ | I | 1 | C * 16 | C * 16 |

# APPENDIX 2

# Fortran IV
# Statement Summary

| Statement | Executable? | Definition number | Page |
|-----------|-------------|-------------------|------|
| A = B | yes | 2.33 | 46 |
| GO TO $N$ | yes | 3.2 | 60 |
| IF $(E) N_1, N_2, N_3$ | yes | 3.3 | 62 |
| GO TO $(N_1, N_2, \ldots, N_m)$,M | yes | 3.4 | 66 |
| GO TO M,$(N_1, N_2, \ldots, N_m)$ | yes | 3.5 | 70 |
| ASSIGN $N$ TO M | yes | 3.6 | 71 |
| STOP $n$ | yes | 3.7 | 72 |
| END | no | 3.8 | 73 |
| READ, $list$ | yes | 4.1 | 80 |
| PRINT, $list$ | yes | 4.2 | 82 |
| FORMAT $(F_1, F_2, \ldots, F_n)$ | no | 4.4 | 86 |
| READ $(5, N)$ $list$ | yes | 4.6 | 87 |
| WRITE $(6, N)$ $list$ | yes | 4.7 | 87 |
| DIMENSION $V(C, C, \ldots, C), V(C, C, \ldots, C), \ldots$ | no | 5.2 | 111 |
| DO $N I = M_1, M_2, M_3$ | yes | 5.3 | 114 |

| *Statement* | *Executable?* | *Definition number* | *Page* |
|---|:---:|:---:|:---:|
| FUNCTION *NAME (ARG*1, *ARG*2, . . . *)* | no | 6.5 | 130 |
| SUBROUTINE *NAME (ARG*1, *ARG*2, . . . *)* | no | 6.8 | 134 |
| CALL *NAME (ARG*1, *ARG*2, . . . *)* | yes | 6.9 | 135 |
| ENTRY *NAME (ARG*1, *ARG*2, . . . *)* | no | 6.10 | 137 |
| EXTERNAL *A, B, C*, . . . | yes | 6.11 | 138 |
| RETURN *I* | no | 6.12 | 140 |
| COMMON */NAME*1/ *A*1, *B*1, . . . */NAME*2/ *A*2, *B*2, . . . | no | 6.13 | 141 |
| EQUIVALENCE $(a1, b1, c1, . . . ), (a2, b2, c2, . . . ), . . .$ | no | 6.14 | 143 |
| DATA *A*1, *B*1, . . . / $n * c1, n * d1$, . . . / , . . . | no | 6.15 | 144 |
| *NAME* (A, B, C, . . . ) = *E* | no | 6.16 | 145 |
| *TYPE* $* S V_1, V_2, V_3$, . . . | no | 7.2 | 151 |
| IMPLICIT *TYPE* $* S (a_1, a_2, . . . ), . . .$ | no | 7.3 | 152 |
| IF *(E) S* | yes | 7.19 | 161 |
| READ *(a, b,* END = *c,* ERR = *d) list* | yes | 8.4 | 181 |
| WRITE *(a, b) list* | yes | 8.5 | 183 |
| REWIND *a* | yes | 8.6 | 184 |
| END FILE *a* | yes | 8.7 | 184 |
| BACKSPACE *a* | yes | 8.8 | 185 |
| DEFINE FILE $a_1 (m_1, r_1, f_1, v_1)$, . . . | no | 8.9 | 186 |
| READ *(a'r, b,* ERR = *d) list* | yes | 8.10 | 187 |
| WRITE *(a'r, b) list* | yes | 8.11 | 188 |
| FIND *(a'r)* | yes | 8.12 | 188 |

# Index